PUSHKIN PRESS

Praise for *Subtly Worded*

'A gifted satirist and social observer… her precise voice is her own and this mercurial volume is a singular prism to not so much a lost world as to a changing culture that learned to adapt without ever forgetting the past'

EILEEN BATTERSBY, *Irish Times*

'Teffi can write in more registers than you might think, and is capable of being heartbreaking as well as very funny. I wish she were still alive, and I could have met her… I can't recommend her strongly enough'

NICHOLAS LEZARD, *Guardian*

'Teffi's brilliance at capturing the dark comedy of her milieu should no longer prevent her from being recognized as an important European writer' *TLS*

'Teffi was not only a great wit and an impeccable stylist, but one of the twentieth century's most perceptive and clear-headed observers'

PEN Atlas

'The characters pop off the page with a flick of the pen. Teffi… turned out finely engraved sentences that achieved their effects economically'

New York Times

Praise for *Memories–From Moscow to the Black Sea*

'I never imagined such a memoir could be possible, especially about the Russian Civil War. Teffi wears her wisdom lightly, observing farce and foible amid the looming tragedy, in this enthralling book'

ANTONY BEEVOR

'A vividly idiosyncratic personal account of the disintegration – moral, political, strategic – of Tsarist Russia after the Revolution, as alive to the farcical and the ridiculous as it is to the tragic; a bit like what Chekhov might have written if he had lived to experience it'

ᴀEL FRAYN

TEFFI (1872–1952) wrote poems, plays, stories, satires and feuilletons, and was renowned in Russia for her wit and powers of observation. Following her emigration in 1919 she settled in Paris, where she became a leading figure in the émigré literary scene. Now her genius has been rediscovered by a new generation of readers, and she once again enjoys huge acclaim in Russia and across the world. Pushkin Press also publishes *Subtly Worded*, a collection of her short stories, and *Memories–From Moscow to the Black Sea*.

ROBERT CHANDLER is a poet and translator best known for his prize-winning translations of Vasily Grossman and Andrey Platonov. He is a co-translator of Teffi's *Subtly Worded* and *Rasputin and Other Ironies*.

ELIZABETH CHANDLER is a co-translator, with Robert Chandler, of Pushkin's *The Captain's Daughter* and of several titles by Andrey Platonov and Vasily Grossman.

ANNE MARIE JACKSON has translated many Russian works and is the editor and co-translator of *Subtly Worded* and Teffi's *Rasputin and Other Ironies*.

ROSE FRANCE is an academic and a translator from Russian. She has translated poems by Lermontov for *After Lermontov: Verses for the Centenary*, and a number of stories and sketches by Teffi and Mikhail Zoshchenko for two forthcoming collections of Russian literature. She teaches Russian language, literature and translation at the University of Edinburgh, and translation at the University of Stirling.

RASPUTIN
AND OTHER IRONIES
BY TEFFI

Edited by
Robert Chandler and Anne Marie Jackson

Translated from the Russian
by Robert Chandler, Elizabeth Chandler,
Rose France and Anne Marie Jackson

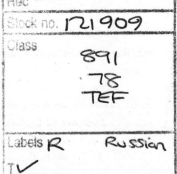
PUSHKIN PRESS
LONDON

Pushkin Press

71–75 Shelton Street, London WC2H 9JQ

Original Russian texts © Agnès Szydlowski

English translations © Rose France, 2016, except: 'My Pseudonym', 'The Gadarene Swine', 'The Merezhkovskys' © Anne Marie Jackson, 2016, 'How I Live and Work', 'Love', 'Ilya Repin' © Robert Chandler, 2016; 'Rasputin', 'My First Tolstoy' © Anne Marie Jackson, 2014, first published in *Subtly Worded* by Pushkin Press in 2014. An earlier version of Robert and Elizabeth Chandler's English translation of 'Love' appeared in *Russian Short Stories from Pushkin to Buida* (London: Penguin Classics, 2005).

'Teffi the Fool' © Robert Chandler, 2016

'A Note on the Texts' © Anne Marie Jackson, 2016

First published by Pushkin Press in 2016

ISBN 978 1 782272 17 5

Set in Monotype Dante by Teragon, London

Printed by CPI Group (UK) Ltd, Croydon, CRO 4YY

www.pushkinpress.com

Contents

CONTENTS

Teffi the Fool

Teffi was a writer of astonishing, fearless intelligence. There was little, if anything, that she did not see through. No other writer, for example, has evoked the plight of the White refugees from "Sovietdom" as vividly, and with such insight, as Teffi in "The Gadarene Swine". In this article, probably her penultimate publication on Russian soil, Teffi lets slip her mask of light humorist—and the result is terrifying. "The Gadarene Swine" was published in Odessa in March 1919, just over a month before the Whites evacuated the city, and it was not republished until 2006. It is hard to imagine any émigré journal intrepid enough to republish anything so mercilessly critical of the Whites.

Teffi was secretive and self-protective. She consistently lied about when she was born, shaving thirteen years off her age. She wrote a substantial amount of apparently autobiographical work, but without ever mentioning several of the most important events of her life. She does not tell us that a jealous admirer shot, and nearly killed, one of her lovers. Nor does she mention her second marriage, nor does she ever speak, even obliquely, of the infant son whom she abandoned when she left her husband to return to Petersburg and begin her career as a writer. All this, of course, is entirely understandable. If it surprises us, it is only because Teffi creates such a powerful illusion, when she writes in the first person, that she is chatting away entirely freely and spontaneously.

Teffi's most important act of self-protection, however, was her adoption of the mask of a fool. Had she written many articles in the vein of "The Gadarene Swine", she would have had few friends and few readers. She understood that intelligence as sharp as hers can be frightening, and, like a Shakespearean fool, she found a way to smuggle her insights into the public world without getting herself executed or lynched. She did this with remarkable skill; she was a true juggler, a tumbler. While in Russia, she wrote exclusively for the liberal press yet was the favourite writer of the last tsar—as well as being admired by Lenin. And many of the sketches she published as an émigrée in Paris were reprinted, without her permission, in Soviet Russia. Few Russian writers of the time were able to cross so many boundaries.

Teffi knew what she was about. In "My Pseudonym" she tells us that she chose as her pseudonym the name of a fool whom she knew—because fools are lucky. This was at a time when pseudonyms were used more often than they are today. But as she herself reminds us, other writers chose names with an obvious message—like Maxim *Gorky*, that is, Maxim *the Bitter*. Or, like Anna Andreyevna *Akhmatova*, they chose names with a dramatic ring. No other major writer chose a name as silly as Teffi.

There were times when Teffi seems to have resented that she had come to be seen exclusively as a comic writer. As early as 1916 she was insisting on the tragic element in her work. And yet she may also have felt that, in order to be able to write at all, she had to pretend—to herself as well as to others—that her writing was nothing so very serious. There is a striking similarity between her account, in "My Pseudonym", of the first night of the very first of her plays to be staged, and her account, in *Memories—From Moscow to the Black Sea*, of the last time she attended a performance of her own work on Russian soil. Both accounts end with a description of an enthusiastic audience calling for "the author" to take her bow and Teffi being unable, or somehow strangely reluctant, to accept the tribute that was her due. It is as if she felt that she might be unable to write at all if she took herself too seriously, that it was better to pretend that her work simply wrote itself.

Teffi's mask served her well. She survived the Russian Civil War, the difficulties of life as an émigrée, and the German occupation of France. She lived to be eighty, continuing to write until her last months. But it is time we reassessed her work, without preconceptions. She is always perceptively witty and she wrote thoughtfully about the power of laughter—but she is not the light humorist that Russians and Russianists still sometimes imagine her to be.

In this volume we present not just one other Teffi, but several. Her range of both tone and subject matter is astonishing. She evokes the inner world of children with as much insight as any writer I know. "Love" is a masterpiece of poetic, modernist prose. She wrote poetry throughout her career and, like several of the very greatest Russian prose writers—Alexander Pushkin, Ivan Bunin, Andrei Platonov and Varlam Shalamov among them—she unobtrusively brings to her prose all that she had learnt as a poet. And her portraits of such figures as Lenin and Rasputin are unforgettable.

Robert Chandler
January 2016

9

A Note on the Texts

Teffi's account of her unplanned emigration from Russia, published in English as *Memories—From Moscow to the Black Sea*, is often seen as her masterpiece. Gathered here is a selection of her shorter reminiscences, ranging from her childhood in 1870s Russia to the Nazi occupation of France in the 1940s.

After she left Russia in 1919, Teffi's longing for that lost world led her to turn to the past in much of her writing. As she puts it in her 1927 collection, *The Small Town (Gorodok)*:

> Our way of life in our ruined Atlantis […] is fading from memory. […] From time to time the sea seems to toss out an unexpected shard, scrap, fragment from this world, this world submerged and lost for evermore, and you begin to examine it with sadness and tenderness, and you remember what the shard used to be like, the whole it was once part of, its role in life—whether to serve, teach, or simply entertain and delight.
>
> And always a shard like this will hook onto your soul and pull it back into the past.

Teffi may also have looked to the past because she felt, as her biographer Edythe Haber describes it, "unable to penetrate the inner life of the French". In a feuilleton in the émigré newspaper *Vozrozhdenie*, Teffi wrote that she would never be able to "speak, think and act" on behalf of a French person the way she could on behalf of a Russian.

The first section of this collection, "How I Live and Work", affords us a few glimpses of Teffi's life as a writer. The pieces in the second section, "Staging Posts" – mostly written in the 1920s – show us something of Teffi's personal life, from childhood and adolescence through to motherhood, emigration and life in Paris. "Staging Posts" itself, the most clearly fictionalized of these writings, alludes to a real episode that also figures in *Memories*, the death of her beloved younger sister Lena; and "The White Flower" evokes Teffi's first years as an émigrée.

Most of the accounts in the final two sections of this volume—"Heady Days: Revolutions and Civil War" and "Artists and Writers Remembered"—come from *My Chronicle*, Teffi's final collection, unpublished during her lifetime. In her preface, Teffi wrote that many interesting people had passed through her life and that her intention was to show them "simply as real people", since few others were likely to portray them this way. "We Are Still Living" and "The Gadarene Swine" were written at the time of the events they describe. The former dates to 1918, before Teffi had left the city she would always call Petersburg, even though after the outbreak of the First World War it had officially been given the more Slavic name of Petrograd, and the latter to the Russian Civil War, when Teffi was "rolling her way down the map", along with thousands of others, before leaving Russia for ever.

Anne Marie Jackson
January 2016

PART I

How I Live and Work

How I Live and Work

Many people find it surprising that I live somewhere so busy, right opposite Montparnasse station. But it's what I like. I adore Paris. I like to hear it here beside me—knocking, honking, ringing and breathing. Sometimes, at dawn, a lorry rumbles past beneath my window so loud and so close that it seems to be coming straight through my room, and I draw up my legs in my sleep so they won't be run over. And then what wakes me an hour or two later is Paris itself—dear, elegant, beautiful Paris. Far better than being woken by some bewhiskered old crone of a concierge, with the eyes of a cockroach.

Many people ask if it's possible for a small pension to provide one with complete comfort. To which I modestly reply, "Well, I wouldn't say quite complete."

Is it this little table you're looking at? Yes, I know it's very small, but there's nothing it doesn't do. It's a writing table, a dining table, a dressing table and a sewing table. It's only three and a half feet across, but on it I have an inkwell, some writing paper, my face powder, some envelopes, my sewing box, a cup of milk, some flowers, a Bible, sweets, manuscripts and some bottles of scent. In layers, like geological strata.

The Augean table. Remember how Hercules had to clean the Augean stables? Well, if Augeas's stables were in such a state, what do you think his writing table would have been like? Probably just like mine. So, how do I write? I put the cup of milk, the Bible and the bottles of scent on the bed, while the sewing box falls of its own accord onto the floor. I need to keep everything essential close at hand—and anyway there's nowhere else to put anything. Though I suppose the flowers could go into the cupboard.

The Bible takes up a quarter of the table, but I need it because Professor Vysheslavtsev, whose outstanding lectures I attend on Mondays (and I recommend everyone else to do the same), often refers to the Epistles of Paul.

So I need to consult the Bible.

Sometimes there are landslides on my table. Everything slips sideways and hangs over the edge. And then it takes only the slightest disturbance of the air (mountaineers will know what I mean); it takes only the opening of a window or the postman knocking at the door—and an entire avalanche roars and crashes to the floor. Sometimes I then discover long-lost items—things I've replaced long ago: gloves; a volume of Proust; a theatre ticket from last summer; an unsent letter (and there I was, impatiently waiting for an answer!); a flower from a ball gown… Sometimes this excites a kind of scientific interest in me, as if I were a palaeontologist who has happened upon the bone of a mammoth. To which era should I assign this glove or page of manuscript?

Worst of all are flowers; if there's a landslide, they create a flood. If someone gives me flowers, they are always taken aback by my look of sudden anxiety.

As for domestic animals, I have only a bead snake and a small monster—a varnished cedar cone standing on little paws. It brings me luck.

While we're on the theme of domesticity and creature comforts, I did also once have a venetian blind. But there wasn't room for it in the room; it had to go. If I'd hung on to it, it could have created mayhem.

I'm not planning to write anything at all big. I think you'll understand why.

We must wait for a big table. And if we wait in vain—*tant pis.*[1]

1926

Translated by Robert and Elizabeth Chandler

My Pseudonym

I'm often asked about the origin of my pseudonym: "Teffi". Why Teffi? It sounds like something you'd call a dog. And a great many readers of the *Russian Word* have indeed given this name to their fox terriers and Italian greyhounds.

And why would a Russian woman sign her work with a name that sounds English?

If I felt I needed a pen name, I could have gone for something with more of a ring to it, or at least a hint of some political ideal, like *bitter* Maxim Gorky, *poor* Demyan Bedny or Skitalets *the Wanderer*. Their names all hint at suffering in the name of some cause and help to win the reader's sympathy.

Besides, women writers tend to go for male pseudonyms. A wise and circumspect move. It is common practice to regard ladies with a somewhat ironic smile, and even with incredulity:

"How on earth did she come up with something like this?"

"Her husband must be doing the writing for her."

Among those women who have used male pseudonyms are the writer known as "Marko Vovchok", the talented novelist and public figure who signed her work as "Vergezhsky" and the talented poetess who writes her critical essays under the name of "Anton the Extreme". All this, I repeat, has its *raison d'être*. It makes sense and it looks good. But "Teffi"? What sort of nonsense is that?

So I'd like to give an honest account of how this literary name came into being. It was as I was taking my first steps in literature. At the time I had published only two or three poems, to which I'd put my own name, and I had also written a little one-act play. I had no idea at all how I was going to get this play on stage. Everyone around me was saying that it was absolutely impossible—I needed to have theatrical connections and a literary name with clout. Otherwise the play would never be staged—and no one would ever even bother to read it.

"What theatre director wants to read just any old nonsense when he could be reading *Hamlet* or *The Government Inspector*? Let alone something concocted by some female!"

At this point I began to do some serious thinking. I didn't want to hide behind a male pseudonym. That would be weak and cowardly. I'd rather use a name that was incomprehensible, neither one thing nor the other.

But what? It had to be a name that would bring good luck. Best of all would be the name of some fool—fools are always lucky.

Finding a fool, of course, was easy enough. I knew a great many of them. But which one should I choose? Obviously it had to be someone very special. Then I remembered a fool who was not only special, but also unfailingly lucky—someone clearly recognized even by fate as the perfect fool.

His name was Stepan, but at home everyone called him Steffi. After tactfully discarding the first letter (so that the fool would not get too big for his boots), I decided to sign my play "Teffi". Then I took a deep breath and sent it straight to the Suvorin

Theatre. I didn't say a word to anyone because I was sure my enterprise would fail.

A month or two went by. I had nearly forgotten about my little play. It had taught me just one thing: that not even fools always bring you good luck.

But then one day in *New Times* I read: *"The Woman Question*, a one-act play by Teffi, has been accepted for production at the Maly Theatre."

I felt terror. Then utter despair.

I could see immediately that my little play was rank nonsense, that it was silly, dull, that you couldn't hide for long behind a pseudonym, and that the play was bound to be a spectacular flop—one that would shame me for the rest of my life. I didn't know what to do, and there was no one I could turn to for advice.

And then I recalled with horror that when I sent the manuscript I had included my name and return address. That wouldn't be a problem if they thought I had sent the package on behalf of somebody else, but what if they guessed the truth? What then?

I didn't have long to think it over. The next day an official letter came in the post, giving me the date of the first night and informing me when rehearsals would start. I was invited to attend.

Everything was out in the open. My lines of retreat had been cut off. This was rock bottom. Since nothing could be more terrifying, I could now give serious thought to my situation.

Why exactly had I decided the play was so very bad? If it was bad, they wouldn't have accepted it. That they had accepted it could only be thanks to the good luck of the fool whose name I had taken. If I had signed the play "Kant" or "Spinoza", they would surely have rejected it.

I needed to pull myself together and go to the rehearsal. Otherwise they might try to track me down through the police.

Along I went. The play was being directed by Yevtikhy Karpov, someone suspicious of any kind of innovation, a man of the old school.

"Box set, three doors, and your lines from memory—rattle them off facing the audience."

He greeted me with condescension. "So you're the author, are you? All right. Find yourself a seat and keep quiet."

Need I say that I did indeed keep quiet? Up on stage a rehearsal was underway. The young actress Grinyova (whom I sometimes still see here in Paris—she has changed so little that when I look at her my heart flutters as it did back then…) was in the lead role. She was holding a crumpled handkerchief that she kept pressing to her mouth—the latest mannerism among young actresses.

"Stop muttering under your breath!" shouted Karpov. "Face the audience! You don't know your lines! You don't know your lines!"

"Yes I do!" said Grinyova, offended.

"Oh do you? All right then. Prompter—not another word from you! Let her stew in her own juice—like a sprat in a pan!"

Karpov was a bad psychologist. No one would remember their lines after intimidation like that.

Oh this is dreadful, I thought, really dreadful! Why had I even written this dreadful play? Why had I sent it to the theatre? The actors were suffering—being forced to learn all this claptrap of mine by heart. And now the play was going to fail and the papers would write, "It is a shame that a serious theatre should be wasting its time on such nonsense when people are going hungry." And then, when I went to my grandmother's for Sunday breakfast, she would give me a stern look and say, "We've been hearing things about you. I very much hope they're untrue."

Nevertheless I carried on going to the rehearsals. I was amazed by the friendly way the actors greeted me—I had expected them to hate and despise me. Karpov laughed loudly and said, "The poor author's wasting away. She's getting thinner and thinner."

The "poor author" held her tongue and tried not to weep. And then came the point of no return. The day of the performance. To go or not to go? I decided to go but to find myself a place somewhere at the very back where no one would see me. After all, Karpov was capable of anything. If the play flopped, he might stick his head out from the wings and shout, "Leave this theatre and don't come back, you fool!"

My little play followed a long and extremely tedious four-act work by some novice. The audience was bored—yawning and whistling its disapproval. Then, after the last jeering whistle and after the interval, up went the curtain and my characters began to prattle away.

"Utterly dreadful!" I was thinking. "What a disgrace!"

But the audience laughed once, laughed again, then began to enjoy themselves. I promptly forgot I was the author and laughed along with everyone else as old Yevgenia Yablochkina played a woman general marching around the stage in uniform and tooting martial fanfares with no instrument but her lips. All in all, the actors were very good. They did my play proud.

"Author!" the audience began calling out. "Author!"

What was I to do?

Up went the curtain. The cast took a bow and made a show of searching for the author.

I leapt from my seat and began to make my way down the aisle towards the wings. Then the curtain came back down, so I returned to my seat. But once again the audience called for the author, and once again the curtain went up, the cast took a bow and someone on stage shouted, "But where's the author?" Once again I made for the wings, but once again the curtain came back down. And so it went on. I carried on dashing backwards and forwards until someone with a shock of wild hair (I learnt later that this was Alexander Kugel) grabbed me by the arm and bellowed, "For the love of God—she's right here!"

But at this point the curtain, after going up for the sixth time, came down once and for all. The audience began to disperse.

The following day I had my first ever conversation with a journalist, who had come to my apartment to interview me.

"What are you working on right now?"

"I'm making some shoes for my niece's doll…"

"Oh really? And what does your pseudonym mean?"

"It's… the name of a foo… I mean it's a surname."

"Someone said it's from Kipling."

Saved! I was saved! There is indeed such a name in Kipling. And not only that, but in *Trilby* there's a little ditty that goes:

> Taffy was a Wale-man,
> Taffy was a thief…[1]

It all came back to me straightaway. Yes, of course, it was from Kipling!

Beneath the photograph of me that appeared in the newspapers was the word "Taffy".[2]

That was it. There was no going back.

And so it remains.

1931
Translated by Anne Marie Jackson

My First Visit to an Editorial Office

M y first steps as an author were terrifying. I had never, in any case, intended to become a writer, even though everyone in our family had written poetry from childhood on. For some reason this activity seemed horribly shameful, and should any of us find a brother or sister with a pencil, a notebook and an inspired expression, we would immediately shout out, "You're writing! You're writing!"

The guilty party would begin to make excuses and the accusers would hop around, jeering, "You're writing! You're writing!"

The only one of us above suspicion was our eldest brother, a creature suffused with sombre irony.[1] But one day, when he was back at the lycée after the summer holidays, we found scraps of paper in his room covered in poetic exclamations, and one line repeated over and over again:

"Oh Mirra, Mirra, palest moon!"

Alas! He, too, was writing poetry.

This discovery made quite an impression on us. And who knows, it may even have influenced my older sister Masha's choice of pen name. When she became famous, she adopted the name "Mirra Lokhvitskaya".

My own dream was to become an artist. I had even, on the advice of a businesslike friend from kindergarten, written this wish down on a piece of paper, chewed it a little, and thrown it out of the window of a train. My kindergarten friend assured me that this was a "foolproof" method.

When my older sister began to publish her own poetry after leaving college, I sometimes went with her to the editorial office on the way back from school. My nanny[2] would come too, carrying my satchel of school books.

And while my sister was sitting in the editor's office (I don't remember now what journal it was, but I remember that the editors were Pyotr Gnedich and Vsevolod Solovyov),[3] Nanny and I would wait in the outer room.

I would sit a little way away from Nanny, so that nobody would guess that she was accompanying me. I would assume an inspired expression, and imagine how everybody—the delivery boy and the copy-typist and all the would-be contributors— would take me for a writer.

The only thing was, the chairs in the reception were inconveniently high, and my feet didn't touch the ground. However, the inspired expression on my face more than made up for this handicap—and for my short dress and school pinafore.

By the age of thirteen, I already had some literary works under my belt. I had written some verses on the arrival of the Tsaritsa[4] and on the anniversary of the founding of our school. These latter—hastily composed in the form of a high-flown ode—contained a stanza for which I was later made to suffer a great deal:

> And may for future generations
> The light of truth shine, like a sun,
> In this great shrine of education,
> For many, many years to come.

My sister tormented me for a whole year over that "great shrine of education". If I pretended I had a headache and wasn't going into school, she would immediately start up a chant: "Nadya, Nadya, why aren't you going to the great shrine of education? How can you bear the light of truth to shine without you?"

And then, when I was sixteen or seventeen, I wrote a comical poem called "The Song of Margarita", and, without showing it to anyone, of course, I decided to take it along to the journal *Oskolki*.

The editor of *Oskolki* was Leikin. At that time he was already very old and in poor health. And he did, in fact, die soon afterwards.

I went to the editorial office. It was terrifying. Particularly when I was on the staircase, about to ring the bell. The door was small and dirty. There was a smell of cabbage pie, something I can't abide. I rang the bell—and thought, "Quick! Run away!"

But then I heard a scrabbling sound from behind the door. Somebody was taking the chain off the hook. The door opened a crack, and an eye peeped through. Then another eye. Then the door opened the rest of the way.

"Who do you want?"

It was a very thin, elderly lady with an Orenburg shawl worn crosswise over her chest.

"I've co-come to-to see Leikin."

"Sir isn't here yet," said the lady. "Come in. Sit down and wait. He will be here presently."

She ushered me into a tiny room and went away. From there I could see another room, also rather small, with a writing desk and, above it, a stuffed bird.

> Above the desk, a stuffed bird
> gawps at the editor without a word.

I waited a long time. Occasionally the lady would come back and, stroking the front of her shawl with her bony hands, would whisper, "Just a little longer. He won't be long now."

Then I heard the doorbell. A stamping of feet, a coughing and a wheezing. I could make out the words:

"Who?"

"What?"

"Eh?"

"Why?"

"For me?"

"Damn!"

Then the wheezing stopped, and once again the thin lady came in and said in a nervous whisper, "Sir still needs to warm up." Then she went out again. I sat and thought how awful it was to lead a literary life.

Once again, the thin lady came in, and, clearly feeling sorry for me and hoping to cheer me up, she whispered, "Sir still hasn't quite warmed up."

Such a kind woman! I wanted to put my arms around her neck, so that we could weep in each other's arms. She went out again. Oh heavens! I so wanted to leave! But I didn't dare leave now. Here she was again, "All over now. He's done."

At first I didn't realize what she meant. For a moment I thought Leikin had died. I got to my feet, horrified.

"Don't fret yourself," said the lady. "Sir will see you now."

I frowned, then stepped forward. After all, he wasn't going to kill me. In an armchair, in front of the stuffed bird, sat a thickset, crook-shouldered, apparently cross-eyed man with a black beard. He seemed very gloomy.

"To what do I owe the honour of this visit?" he asked, not looking at me. "What do you want?"

"Poetry," I mumbled.

"What poetry?"

"'The Song of Margarita'."

"Eh? I don't think we've ever had that here. Can you give me a clearer idea of what you mean?"

"I wrote it. Here it is."

He held out his hand, still not looking at me. I thrust my sheet of paper into it.

"Well?" he said.

"What?" I asked.

"Well—goodbye. You'll be able to read the answer in our 'post bag'."[5]

A month later, I read in the *Oskolki* "post bag": "'The Song of Margarita' has nothing to recommend it."

This was my first step as a writer. Later, by way of a secret triumph over that angry (albeit by then deceased) editor, I managed to get it printed no fewer than four times, in a number of publications.

Though, I think, had I been an editor myself, I wouldn't have printed it even once.

1929
Translated by Rose France

PART II

Staging Posts

Liza

The three of us were sitting together: I, my sister Lena, and Liza, the priest's daughter,[1] who used to come to our house to have lessons, and compete with us to be seen as the most diligent and obedient pupil.

Today there were no lessons and we were not allowed to play. Today was a solemn, anxious day—Holy Saturday.[2]

We had to sit quietly, not bother or pester anybody, not fight, and not fidget or kneel on our chairs. Everything was difficult, complicated and extremely disagreeable. The shadow of pain and mortification hung over the entire day.

Everyone was busy, irritable, in a hurry. Our governess with the red blotches on her cheeks was running up a blouse for herself on the sewing machine. Huh! As if it made any difference to her pockmarked nose. Nanny had gone into the big girls' room to iron pinafores. My elder sisters were sitting in the dining room, decorating eggs. They greeted me in their usual way: "The very last person we want in here! Won't you take her away, Nanny?"

I tried to stand my ground but promptly knocked over a cup of paint with my elbow, and, with the assistance of Nanny, who came bustling in, was returned to the nursery. And in the midst of this debacle I found out that our parents wouldn't be taking us to church that evening for the Easter Vigil.

I was so furious I didn't even cry. I just said sardonically, "We get dragged along for confession all right. They take the best—and leave the worst for us."

Despite my brilliant rejoinder, the enemy prevailed; we had to retreat to the nursery.

Just then, as ill luck would have it, Lena and I were in the midst of a heated theological debate—on the subject of robbers and prayers. The priest had told us that before beginning any task, we should always say a prayer. I was immediately struck by a difficult problem: when a robber is about to kill someone, shouldn't he say a prayer first? After all, killing is his task. But Lena argued that a robber didn't need to say a prayer first, since he'd be forgiven for all his sins in one go.

There was no one we could ask, and we weren't allowed to fight. What could we do?

At last, Liza arrived.

Liza had a thin, taut face. Her big, pale, bulging eyes always bore a look of startled inspiration. She saw everything two or three times larger than life, and told lies as if she lied for a living.

She was a year older than me. She had already been twice to confession. Lena and I looked on her with respect.

We knew every detail about Liza's home life, all of which was quite fascinating.

Liza had an uncle, a seminary student, Pyotr Yakovlevich, who had once drunk the milk of four cows. He had arrived to find no one at home and all the milk from that evening's milking standing in the porch, and he had drunk the lot.

Also, Liza's family had four golden grand pianos at home, but they were hidden in the hayloft, so that nobody could see them.

Also, nobody ever ate dinner at Liza's house. Instead, there was a big cupboard in the hall that was always full of roast chickens. If anyone was hungry, all he had to do was to poke his head into the cupboard, eat a chicken and go on his way.

Also, Liza had fourteen velvet dresses, but she only wore them at night so that nobody would see them. In the daytime she hid them in the kitchen under the big pot they used for making pastry.

Also, Liza spoke very good French, but not the kind of French we spoke with our governess. Liza spoke a different kind of French, which nobody understood.

All in all, Liza's life was quite fascinating.

So there we were, sitting quietly and talking. Liza was telling us her news. First, we had to cross our hearts and swear not to tell a soul.

We crossed our hearts and swore. To make it still more binding, we spat over our left shoulders.

"You promise not to tell a soul?"

"Not a soul, for ever and ever, Amen."

Liza shot a glance at the door, her eyes pale and terrible, and whispered, "The wife of Trifon the gardener gave birth to two puppies and told everyone they were children, but when people started to ask questions, she roasted them and gave them to Trifon to eat."

"But you can't eat puppies," said Lena in fright. "It's a sin."

"But she never told anyone they were puppies. She told everyone they were children."

TEFFI

I felt my hands grow cold. And Liza was frightened too; she had tears in her eyes and her nose was all swollen: "It was the Devil got into her. Everyone knows it's easy for the Devil to creep up on people when they're asleep."

"Have you ever seen the Devil, Liza?"

"Yes. Evening's the time to look out for him. If the cross round your neck suddenly shines very bright, that means the Devil will definitely come."

"So you've seen him?"

"Yes, I've seen him. If I wake up in the night and I poke my head out of the bedclothes, I always see a devil over Papa's head, and a devil over Mama's head. Papa and Mama both have a devil standing over them all night long."

"And black cats, too," I said. "Black cats are full of it too."

"Full of what?"

"Full of the Devil. If a black cat crosses your path, something bad will definitely happen to you."

"Even a black hare can be dangerous," added Lena.

I was genuinely surprised. How did my little sister know this without me telling her?

"Yes, very dangerous," agreed Liza. "When our Lida was dying I went with my Aunt Katya to Lichevka to buy some muslin. On our way back, a black cat ran across the road. And then, all of a sudden, a hare! And then a wolf! And then a bear! And then a tiger! And a mole! And when we got back, Lidochka was already dead."

I was so excited that for some time now I had been kneeling on my chair with my elbows on the table.

"Oh, that's so awful, Liza," I said. "Though, you know, I'm not afraid of anything—not really. I'm only afraid of wolves.

36

And ghosts. And dark rooms. And dead people. I'm awfully afraid of dead people. And sleeping in a room all by myself. And I'd never go out in the forest alone. But apart from that, I'm not afraid of anything. If someone gave me a gun for Easter, I'd shoot the lot of them straightaway, right in the head. Just like that! I'm not afraid of anything."

"So, what are you getting for Easter?" asked Liza.

"I don't know. A croquet set, maybe. What about you?"

"I'm getting—a croquet set too, and a… grand piano."

"But I thought you already had some grand pianos!"

"Yes, but we need more. And then, I'm getting a carriage. And a gold-plated tin of sardines. And gold-embroidered slippers. And a golden comb. And a golden spoon."

Lucky Liza. Everything she has is made of gold.

"Liza, why is it you always smell of onion? And smoke?"

"Oh, that's the eau de cologne we use."

Lena gawped at Liza. But I knew that there were different kinds of eau de cologne, made with different flowers and herbs. Clearly, Liza's family used eau de cologne made with onion.

"Are you going to the Easter Vigil?" Liza asked suddenly.

Oh. That was the question I had been dreading. All through Good Friday we had been talking about the Vigil and what dresses we'd be given to wear. We were so hoping it would be our light blue ones.

I pretended I hadn't heard. But then, to my amazement, I heard Lena answering calmly, "We don't know yet. It depends on the weather."

Clever Lena! I'd never have come up with that myself.

"Aunt Sonia said that last year she was in Arkhangelsk at Easter, and it snowed," I said, doing my bit to salvage our dignity.

"My mama told me," remarked Liza with an astonishing lack of tact, "that your parents aren't taking you to church this year."

Nanny came in with a pile of freshly ironed pinafores over one arm. With her free hand, she slapped her hip indignantly.

"Look at this one, kneeling again! She's worn all the legs of her stockings to holes. How on earth am I meant to keep up with the darning?"

"This one", of course, was me.

To obey immediately and get down from the chair would be demeaning. I slowly lowered one leg, as if of my own accord.

"Well, are you getting down from the chair or not?" exclaimed Nanny impatiently. "Whatever I say it's like water off a duck's back! Liza, put your coat on, your auntie's come for you."

Liza got up. Now it was safe to get down from the chair.

Liza tied a woollen shawl around her head. With a sideways glance at Nanny, she whispered, "Your nanny doesn't have feathers in her eiderdown, she has three million roubles hidden in there, in gold coins. And it's no secret—the robbers all know."

In her dark shawl Liza's face looked thin and pale. What she had just said made me feel afraid for Nanny. Lena's bottom lip began to twist and wobble from side to side. She was about to cry.

Liza glanced quickly again at Nanny, out of the corner of her eye, as if to warn us to keep our mouths shut.

She left. Lena and I were now on our own. Neither of us said anything.

After Liza's visits, everything felt somehow special, mysterious and unsettling.

The thin branches of the cherry tree, already green with buds, stirred restlessly outside the window, peering into the room.

The blanket on Nanny's bed also seemed to be stirring. Maybe a robber had got in and was now lying hidden under the blanket, stealing the gold...

1927
Translated by Rose France

Love

It was the wonderful days of my ninth spring—days that were long and full to the brim, saturated with life.

Everything in those days was interesting, important and full of meaning. Objects were new. And people were wise; they knew an astonishing amount and were keeping their great dark secrets until some unknown day in the future.

The morning of each long day began joyfully: thousands of small rainbows in the soapy foam of the wash bowl; a new, brightly coloured light dress; a prayer before the icon, behind which the stems of pussy willow were still fresh; tea on a terrace shaded by lemon trees that had been carried out from the orangery in their tubs; my elder sisters, black-browed and with long plaits, only just back from boarding school for the holidays and still seeming strange to me; the slap of washing bats from the pond beyond the flower garden, where the women doing the laundry were calling out to one another in ringing voices; the languid clucking of hens behind a clump of young, still small-leaved lilac. Not only was everything new and joyful in itself but it was, moreover, a promise of something still more new and joyful.

And it was during this spring, the ninth of my life, that my first love came, revealed itself and left—in all its fullness, with rapture and pain and disenchantment, with all that is to be expected of any true love.

Four peasant girls, Khodoska, Paraska, Pidorka and Khovra—all wearing coin necklaces, Ukrainian wraparound skirts and linen shirts with embroidered shoulders—were weeding the garden paths. They scraped and hacked at the fresh black earth with their spades, turning over thick, oily sods and tearing away crackly, tenacious rootlets as thin as nerves.

For hours on end, until I was called, I would stand and watch, and breathe in the heavy damp smell of the earth.

Necklaces dangled and clinked, arms red from the year's first strong sun slid lightly and gaily up and down the spades' wooden handles.

And then one day, instead of Khovra, who was fair and stocky, with a thin red band around her head, I saw a new girl—tall and lithe, with narrow hips.

"Hey, new girl, what's your name?" I asked.

A dark head encircled by thick, four-stranded plaits and with a narrow white parting down the centre turned towards me, and dark, mischievous eyes looked at me from beneath curved eyebrows that met in the middle, and a merry red mouth smiled at me.

"Ganka!"

And her teeth gleamed—even, white and large.

She said her name and laughed, and the other girls all laughed, and I felt merry too.

This Ganka was astonishing. Why was she laughing? And what was it about her that made me feel so merry? She was not as well dressed as smart Paraska, but her thick striped skirt was wound so deftly round her shapely hips, her red woollen sash gripped her waist so firmly and vibrantly and her bright green ribbon fluttered so arrestingly by the collar of her shirt that it was hard to imagine anything prettier.

I looked at her, and every move, every turn of her supple dark neck sang like a song in my soul. And her eyes flashed again, mischievous, as if tickling me; they laughed, then looked down.

I also felt astonished by Paraska, Khodoska and Pidorka— how could they keep their eyes off her? How did they dare behave as if they were her equals? Were they blind? But then even she herself seemed to think she was no different from the others.

I looked at her fixedly, without thoughts, as if dreaming.

From far away a voice called my name. I knew I was being called to my music lesson, but I didn't answer.

Then I saw Mama going down a nearby avenue with two smartly dressed ladies I didn't know. Mama called to me. I had to go and drop a curtsy to them. One of the ladies lifted my chin with a little hand sheathed in a perfumed white glove. She was gentle, all in white, all in lace. Looking at her, I suddenly felt Ganka was coarse and rough.

"No, Ganka's not nice," I thought.

I wandered quietly back to the house.

Placid, merry and carefree, I went out the following morning to see where the girls were weeding now.

Those sweet dark eyes met me as gaily and affectionately as if nothing had happened, as if I had never betrayed them for a perfumed lady in lace. And again the singing music of the movements of her slender body took over, began to enchant.

The conversation at breakfast was about yesterday's guest, Countess Mionchinskaya. My eldest brother was sincerely enraptured by her. He was straightforward and kind but, since he was being educated at the lycée, he felt it necessary to lisp and drawl and slightly drag his right foot as he walked.[1] And, doubtless afraid that a summer deep in the country might erase these stigmata of the dandy, he greatly surprised us younger ones with his strange mannerisms.

"The countess is divi-i-inely beau-utiful!" he said. "She was the to-oast of the se-ea-son."

My other brother, a cadet at the military academy, did not agree. "I don't see anything so special about her. She may put on airs, but she's got the mitts of a peasant—the mitts of a *baba* who's been soaking neckweed."[2]

The first brother poured scorn on this: "*Qu'est-ce que c'est* mitt? *Qu'est-ce que c'est* baba? *Qu'est-ce que c'est* neckweed?"

"But I'll tell you who really *is* a beauty," the second brother continued, "and that's Ganka who works in the garden."

"Hah!"

"She's badly dressed, of course, but give her a lace gown and gloves and she'll beat your countess hands down."

My heart started beating so fast I had to close my eyes.

"How can you talk such rubbish?" said my sister Vera, taking offence on the countess's behalf. "Ganka's coarse, and she has no manners. She probably eats fish with a knife."

I was in torment. It seemed as if something, some secret of mine, was about to be revealed—but what this secret was I did not even know myself.

"Although that, I think we can say, has nothing to do with it," said the first brother. "Helen of Troy didn't have French

43

governesses, and she ate fish with her fingers—not even with a knife—yet her renown as a world beauty remains unchallenged. What's the matter, Kishmish? Why have you gone so red?"

"Kishmish" was my nickname.[3] I answered in a trembling voice, "Leave me in peace. I'm not doing you any harm. But you... you're always picking on me."

In the evening, lying on the sofa in the dark drawing room, I heard my mother in the hall; she was playing a piece I loved, the cavatina from the opera *Martha*.[4] Something in the soft, tender melody evoked—called up within me—the same singing languor that I had seen in Ganka's movements. And this sweet torment, and the music, and my sadness and happiness made me cry, burying my face in a cushion.

It was a grey morning, and I was afraid it would rain and I wouldn't be allowed out into the garden.

I was, indeed, not allowed out.

I sat down sadly at the piano and began playing exercises, stumbling each time in the same place.

But later in the morning the sun appeared and I raced out into the garden.

The girls had just thrown down their spades and sat down for their midday meal. They got out pots and jugs wrapped in cloths and began to eat. One was eating buckwheat kasha, another had some soured milk. Ganka unwrapped her own little bundle, took out a thick crust of bread and a bulb of garlic, rubbed the bread with the garlic and began to eat, shining her mischievous eyes at me.

I took fright and went away. How terrible that Ganka ate such filth. It was as if the garlic had thrust her away from me.

She had become alien and incomprehensible. Better if she'd eaten fish with a knife.

I remembered what my brother had said about Yelena the Beautiful,[5] but this brought me no consolation and I plodded back to the house.

Nanny was sitting by the back door, knitting a stocking and listening to the housekeeper.

I heard the name "Ganka" and froze. I knew only too well that if I went up to them they'd either shoo me away or stop talking.

"She worked for the steward's wife all winter. She's a hard-working girl. But not an evening went by—the steward's wife noticed—without a soldier coming to see her. The steward's wife packed him off once, and she packed him off twice—but what could the good woman do? She couldn't be packing him off night after night."

"Indeed!" said Nanny. "How could she?"

"So she scolded her now and again, of course, but Ganka just laughed—it was water off a duck's back. Then, just before Twelfth Night, the steward's wife hears noises in the kitchen—as if Ganka were constantly pushing something about the room. And then, first thing in the morning, she hears tiny squeals. She hurries into the kitchen: not a sign of Ganka—just a baby wrapped up in pieces of cloth, lying on some bedding and letting out little squeals. She takes fright. She looks everywhere: where was Ganka? Had something very bad happened? She looks out through the window—and there she is. Standing by the hole in the ice, barefoot, washing out her linen and singing away. The steward's wife would have liked to dismiss her, but how could she manage without her? It's not easy to find such a sturdy, hard-working lass."

I slipped quietly off.

So Ganka was friends with a common, uneducated soldier. This was horrible, horrible. And then she had tormented some little baby. This really was something dark and terrible. She had stolen it from somewhere and wrapped it up in rags; and when it had begun to squeal, she'd run off to the ice hole and sung songs there.

All evening I was in misery. That night I had a dream from which I awoke in tears. But my dream was neither sad nor frightening, and I was crying not from grief but from rapture. When I woke, I could barely remember it. I could only say, "I dreamt of a boat. It was quite transparent, light blue. It floated through the wall, straight into silver rushes. Everything was poetry and music."

"So why all the howling?" asked Nanny. "It's only a boat! Maybe this boat of yours will bring you something good."

I could see she didn't understand, but there was nothing more I could say or explain. And my soul was ringing, singing, weeping in ecstasy. A light-blue boat, silver rushes, poetry and music.

I didn't go out into the garden. I was afraid I'd see Ganka and begin thinking about the soldier and the little baby wrapped up in cloth, that everything would once again become frightening and incomprehensible.

The day dragged restlessly on. It was blustery outside and the wind was bending the trees. The branches shook; the leaves made a dry, boiling sound, like sea surf.

In the corridor, outside the store room, was a surprise: on the table stood an opened crate of oranges. It must have been brought from town that morning; after lunch they'd be handed out to us.

I adore oranges. They are round and golden, like the sun, and beneath their peel are thousands of tiny pockets bursting with sweet, fragrant juice. An orange is a joy. An orange is a thing of beauty.

And suddenly I thought of Ganka. She didn't know about oranges. Warm tenderness and pity filled my heart.

Poor Ganka! She didn't know. I must give her one. But how? To take one without asking was unthinkable. But if I did ask, I'd be told to wait until after lunch. And then I wouldn't be able to take the orange away from table. I wouldn't be allowed to, or they'd ask questions—someone might even guess. I'd be laughed at. Better just to take one without asking. I'd be punished, I wouldn't be given any more—but so what? What was I afraid of?

Round, cool and pleasing, the orange lay in my hand.

How could I? Thief! Thief! Never mind. There'd be time enough for all that—what mattered now was to find Ganka.

The girls turned out to be weeding right by the house, by the back door.

"Ganka! This is for you, for you! Try it—it's for you."

Her red mouth laughed.

"What is it?"

"It's an orange. It's for you."

She turned it round and round in her hand. I mustn't embarrass her.

I ran back inside and, sticking my head out of the corridor window, waited to see what would happen. I wanted to share in Ganka's delight.

She bit off a piece together with the peel (Oh, why hadn't I peeled it first?), then suddenly opened her mouth wide, made a horrible face, spat everything out and hurled the orange far into the bushes. The other girls stood around her, laughing. And she was still screwing up her face, shaking her head, spitting, and wiping her mouth with the cuff of her embroidered shirt.

I climbed down from the windowsill and went quickly to the dark end of the corridor. Squeezing behind a large chest covered with a dusty carpet, I sat on the floor and began to weep.

Everything was over. I had become a thief in order to give her the best thing I knew in all the world. And she hadn't understood, and she had spat it out.

How would I ever survive this grief and this hurt?

I wept till I had no more tears. Then a new thought came into my head: "What if there are mice here behind the chest?"

This fear entered my soul, grew in strength, scared away my previous feelings and returned me to life.

In the corridor I bumped into Nanny. She threw up her hands in horror.

"Your dress! Your dress! You're covered in muck, head to toe! And don't tell me you're crying again, are you?"

I said nothing. This morning humanity had failed to understand my silver rushes, which I had so longed to explain. And "this"—this was beyond telling. "This" was something I had to be alone with.

But humanity wanted an answer. It was shaking me by the shoulder. And I fended it off as best I could.

"I'm not crying. I... my... I've just got toothache."

1924
Translated by Robert and Elizabeth Chandler

The Green Devil

I could think of nothing else all month: Would they let me go to the Christmas party, or not?

I was cunning. I prepared the ground. I told my mother about the glorious achievements of Zhenya Ryazanova, for whom the party was being given. I said that Zhenya was doing very well at school, that she was almost top of the class and was always being held up as an example to us. And that she wasn't just a little girl, but a very serious woman: she was already sixteen.

In short, I didn't waste any time. And then, one fine morning I was called into the living room and told to stand in front of the big mirror and try on a white dress with a blue sash; I understood that I had won. I would be going to the party.

After that, preparations began in earnest: I took oil from the icon lamp in Nanny's room and smeared it on my eyebrows every evening to make them grow thicker in time for the ball; I altered a corset my older sister had thrown away and then hid it under the mattress; I rehearsed sophisticated poses and enigmatic smiles in front of the mirror. My family expressed surprise. "Why's Nadya looking so idiotic?" people kept asking. "I suppose she's at that awkward age. Oh well, she'll grow out of it."

The Christmas party would be on the 24th. Zhenya's name day.

I did everything in my power on the aesthetic front. With no resources at my disposal but a torn corset, I still managed to achieve a quite extraordinary effect. I cinched myself in so tight at the waist that I could only stand on tiptoe. I could barely breathe, and my face took on an imploring look. But it was a joy to make my first sacrifices in the name of beauty.

Nanny was to take me to the party. I put on my fur coat before saying goodbye to my family, so as not to overwhelm them with my shapeliness.

There were a lot of people at the Ryazanovs, and most of them grown up: officers, friends of Zhenya's brother, ladies of various ages. There were only two or three younger girls like myself, and only one cadet between us, so we had to dance with the officers. This was a great honour, of course, but a little intimidating.

At dinner, despite all my attempts to manoeuvre myself into the place next to the cadet, I was seated beside a large officer with a black beard. He was probably about thirty, but at the time he seemed to me a decrepit creature whose life was behind him.

"A fine old relic to be sitting next to," I thought. "Seems I'm in for a jolly evening!"

The officer studied me very seriously and said, "You're a typical Cleopatra. Quite remarkable."

Alarmed, I said nothing.

"I just said," he went on, "that you remind me of Cleopatra. Have you done Cleopatra at school yet?"

"Yes."

"You have her regal air, and you are just as sophisticated and experienced a flirt. The only thing is, your feet don't touch the ground. But that's a minor detail."[1]

My heart beat faster. That I was an experienced flirt, I had no doubt. But how had this old man spotted it so very quickly?

"Look inside your napkin," he said.

I looked. A pink chenille ballerina was poking out of the napkin.

"Look what I have."

He had a green devil, with a tail made from silver metallic cord. The tail shook and the devil danced on a wire, so jolly and so beautiful that I gasped and reached my hand out towards it.

"Stop it!" he said. "He's my devil! You have a ballerina. Tell her how pretty she is!"

He stood the devil in front of his plate.

"Look at him. Isn't he wonderful? I can honestly say he's the finest work of art I've ever seen. Still, I don't suppose you're interested in art. You're a flirt. A Cleopatra. You just want to lure men to their doom."

"Yes, he really is the very most handsome," I babbled. "Nobody else has anyone like him."

The officer briskly inspected the other guests. Everybody had a small chenille figure: a dog wearing a skirt, a chimney-sweep, a monkey. Nobody had a devil like he did. Or anything the least bit like him.

"Well, of course, a devil like him doesn't come along every day of the week. Look at his tail. It shakes all by itself—without anyone even touching it. And he's such a jolly little fellow!"

There was no need to tell me all this. I was already very taken with the devil. So much so that I didn't even feel like eating.

"Why aren't you eating? Did your mother tell you not to?"

Ugh, how very rude! What did my mother have to do with it, when I was a society woman dining with an officer at a ball?

"No, *merci*, I just don't feel like it. I never eat much at balls."

"Really? Well, *you* know what's best for you—you must have been to lots of balls over the years. But why aren't you looking at my little devil? You won't be able to admire him much longer, you know. Dinner will be over soon and I'll be putting him in my pocket and going back home with him."

"What will you do with him?" I asked, with timid hope.

"What do you mean? He will bring beauty to my lonely life. And then I'll get married and show him to my wife, if she's well-behaved. He's a wonderful little devil, isn't he?"

Horrid old, mean old man, I thought. Didn't he understand how I loved that jolly devil? How I *loved* him!

If he hadn't been so delighted with the devil himself, I might have suggested a swap. My ballerina for his devil. But he was so entranced with this devil that there seemed no point in pestering him.

"Why are you so sad all of a sudden?" he asked. "Is it because all this will be over soon? And you'll never again see anything like him? It's true, you don't come across his sort so very often."

I hated this unkind man. I even refused a second helping of ice cream, which I really wanted. I refused because I was very unhappy. Nothing in the world mattered to me any more. I had no use for any of life's pleasures and believed in nothing.

Everyone got up from the table. And my companion hurried off, too. But the little devil was still there on the table. I waited. Not that I was thinking anything in particular. I wasn't thinking with my head. It seemed that only my heart was thinking, because it began to beat fast and hard against the top of my tight corset.

The officer didn't come back.

I took the devil. The springy silver tail whipped against my hand. Quick—into my pocket he went.

They were dancing again in the hall. The nice young cadet asked me for a dance. I didn't dare. I was afraid the devil would jump out of my pocket.

I didn't love the devil any more. He had not brought me joy. Only worry and anxiety. Perhaps I just needed to take a quick look at him—then I'd be ready to suffer for his sake. But as it was... What had I gone and done? Should I just slip in and put him back on the table? But the dining room door was locked now. Probably they were already clearing the table.

"Why are you looking so sad, my charming lady?"

The "old man" was standing beside me, smiling roguishly. "I've suffered a real tragedy," he said. "My devil's gone missing. I'm at my wit's end. I'm going to ring the police. They need to carry out a search. There may be a dangerous criminal in our midst."

He smiled. What he said about the police was, of course, a joke.

"How old are you?" he asked suddenly.

"I'll be fifteen soon. In ten months."

"Aha! As soon as that! So in three years' time I could be marrying you. If only my dear little devil hadn't disappeared so inexplicably. How will I be able to make my wife happy now? Why are you so silent? Do you think I'm too old for you?"

"Not now," I answered gloomily. "But in three years' time you'll be an important general."

"A general. That's a nice thought. But what can have happened to my devil?"

I looked up into his face. I hated him so much and I was so hugely unhappy that he stopped smiling and walked away.

And I went to my friend's room and, hiding behind the curtain (not that there was anyone else in the room), I took out the devil. He was a little squashed, but there was something else besides. He had changed. Looking at him no longer made me feel the least bit happy. I didn't want to touch him, and I didn't want to laugh. He was just the most ordinary devil, green chenille with a little silver tail. How could he make anybody happy? How ridiculous it all was!

I stood up on the window sill, opened the small pane at the top and threw him out on the street.

Nanny was waiting for me in the hall.

The officer walked up to us, glanced at Nanny and chuckled: "Here to collect our Queen Cleopatra, are you?"

And then he fell silent, looked at me thoughtfully and said, simply and kindly, "Off you go. Off to bed with you, little one. You've gone quite pale. God bless you."

I said goodbye and left, quiet and tired.

B-o-r-i-n-g.[2]

1925
Translated by Rose France

Valya

I was in my twenty-first year.
She, my daughter, was in her fourth.[1]

We were not well matched.

I was rather nervy and unpredictable at that time, usually either crying or laughing.

Valya, on the other hand, was very even-tempered and calm. And from morning to night she was engaged in commerce—bargaining with me for chocolates.

In the morning she would not get up until she was given a chocolate. Nor would she go out for a walk, come back from a walk, have breakfast, have lunch, drink milk, get into the bath, get out of the bath, sleep or comb her hair except for a fee—a chocolate. Without chocolate, all life would come to a standstill, all activity replaced by a deafening, systematic howl. Then I would feel I was a monster, a child-killer. And I would give in to her.

Valya despised me for my lack of good sense—that was clear enough. But she didn't treat me too badly. Sometimes she would even pet me with her soft, warm hand, which was always sticky from sweets.

"You're so pretty," she would say. "You have a nose like my elly-phant."

Not particularly flattering. But I knew that my daughter thought her little rubber elephant more beautiful than the Venus de Milo. We all have our different ideals. So I was happy to hear her say this, although I tried not to encourage endearments from her when there were other people around.

Apart from sweets, Valya was interested in very little. Though once, while drawing moustaches on some elderly aunts in a photograph album, she asked in passing, "So where is Jesus Christ now?"

And, without waiting for an answer, she demanded a chocolate.

She was very strict about decorum. She insisted on being the first to be greeted by everyone. On one occasion she came up to me very upset and indignant indeed: "Motya the cook's daughter has gone out on the balcony in only her skirt," she said. "And there are *geese* out there."

Yes, she was very punctilious.

It seemed that year as if Christmas would be a rather sad, anxious time. Sometimes I was able to laugh, since I wanted so badly to live on God's earth. But more often I cried, since life was proving almost beyond me.

For days on end Valya talked with her little elephant about a Christmas tree. It was clear that I would have to get hold of one.

In secret, I ordered some Dresden ornaments from Muir and Mirrielees.[2] I unpacked them at night.

They were absolutely wonderful: little houses and lanterns, parrots in golden cages. But best of all was a little angel, all covered in gold glitter, with iridescent mica wings. The angel hung on a piece of elastic and its wings fluttered when it moved.

What the angel was made of, I don't know. It could have been wax. It had pink cheeks and it held a rose in its hands. I had never seen anything so marvellous.

And at once I thought, "Better not hang it on the tree. In any case its beauty will be lost on Valya. She'll only break it. I'll keep it for myself."

So that's what I decided to do.

But in the morning, Valya sneezed. She must have caught a cold, I thought. I was seized with anxiety.

She might look chubby, but that didn't mean she wasn't delicate. I didn't take good enough care of her. I was a bad mother. And now, wanting to keep the best for myself, I'd hidden the angel. "Its beauty will be lost on her," I had said to myself. But if that were the case, it was only because I hadn't taught her to appreciate beauty.

On the night before Christmas, when I was decorating the tree, I took out the angel. I looked at it for a long time. What a pretty little thing it was, with that rose in its chubby little hand. It looked so cheerful, so rosy-cheeked, yet so gentle. An angel like that should be hidden away in a box, and only on bad days—when the postman brought me horrid letters, and the lamps burned low and the wind made the roof rattle— only then should I allow myself to take it out, to dangle it gently on its elastic and watch the glitter of the gold and the play of light on the mica wings. This might not sound like much. It might sound sad. But did I have anything better to look forward to?

I hung the angel high up on the tree. It was the most beautiful of all the ornaments, so it had to be in the place of honour. But all the time there was another thought in my head—a secret, mean thought. High up, it would be less obvious to *smaller persons*.

That evening we lit the candles on the tree. We invited Motka, and Lyoshka, the laundrywoman's son. And Valya was so sweet and affectionate that my hard heart began to melt. I lifted her up in my arms and I showed her the angel.

"An angel?" she said in her businesslike way. "Give it to me."

I gave it to her.

She looked at it for a long time, stroking its wings with one finger.

I saw that she liked the angel, and I felt proud of my daughter. After all, she hadn't paid the least attention to the stupid clown, even though it was so brightly coloured.

Valya suddenly bent forward and kissed the angel. My darling girl!

At that moment Niushenka, one of our neighbours, arrived. She had brought a gramophone with her. We began to dance.

Really I ought to hide the angel, I thought. It'll only get broken… But where was Valya?

Valya was standing in the corner behind the bookshelf. Her mouth and cheeks were smeared with something raspberry-coloured. She looked troubled.

"What is it, Valya? What's the matter? What's that in your hand?"

In her hand were the mica wings, crumpled and broken.

"It tasted a bit sweet," she said.

I must wash her at once, I thought. I must scrub her tongue. That was what mattered—the paint might be poisonous. She seemed, thank God, to be all right. But why was I crying as I threw the broken mica wings in the fire? How very silly of me! I was crying!

Valya stroked me indulgently on the cheek with her soft hand, which was warm and sticky, and tried to comfort me:

"Don't cry, you silly. I'll buy you some money."

1926
Translated by Rose France

Staging Posts

I

O n that morning it was always sunny.

The weather was always bright and cheerful. So, at least, both Liza and Katya remembered it for the rest of their lives.[1]

On that morning, Nanny would always dress them in new, light-coloured dresses. Then she would go to the "big" dining room, where the adults were drinking tea, and come back up again with half a hard-boiled egg, a piece of *kulich* and a piece of *paskha*[2] for each of them.

Nanny herself always broke her Lenten fast early in the morning when she came back from the Liturgy. She would have cream with her coffee, and the children knew that she would grumble all day and start to feel out of sorts by evening.

The hard-boiled egg would always get stuck somewhere in Liza's chest and they would have to pummel her hard on the back to dislodge it.

The housekeeper, who on that day always smelt of vanilla, would come to wish them a happy Easter.

And she would tell them the story of how, twenty years ago, the mistress of a certain house had made a *baba*[3] using beaten egg white, and how the *baba* had "fallen in the oven". And the mistress had strung herself up from the shame of it.

Liza knew this story, but she could never work out which of the two women had strung herself up and which had fallen into the oven: the baba or the mistress? She imagined a huge blazing oven, like the "fiery furnace" in the holy pictures into which the three youths were thrown.[4] And she imagined a great fat *baba*—the mistress—falling into the oven. In short, she couldn't make head nor tail of it, but it was clearly something horrid, even though the housekeeper told the story cheerfully, with relish.

The housekeeper would also always reminisce about a certain August Ivanovich, a gentleman she had once worked for.

"Would you believe it—a German and all, but such a religious man he was! All through Holy Week he wouldn't take a bite of meat. 'It will taste all the better when I break my fast on Easter morning,' he used to say. A German and all, but he would never sit down to Easter breakfast without ham on the table—not for all the world. That's how religious he was!"

In the evening Liza remembered something very important, went along to her elder sister and said, "Last year, you told me you were already a growing girl, and I was still a child. But this year I fasted for Lent, so that means I'm a growing girl now too."

Her sister turned away, annoyed, and muttered, "You may be a growing girl, but I'm a young lady. Anyway, you should be in the nursery. Go away, or I'll tell Mademoiselle."

Liza pondered these words bitterly. She would never catch up with Masha. In four years' time she herself might be a young lady, but by then, Masha would already be an old maid. She would never catch up with her.[5]

2

The church is crowded and stuffy. Candles splutter quietly in the hands of the worshippers. A pale blue blanket of incense smoke is spread out high in the dome. Down below—the gold of the icons, black figures and the flames of the candles. All around—black, candlelight and gold.

Liza is tired. She breaks off pieces of melted wax, rolls them into pellets and sticks them back onto the candle, noting how much of the Gospel the priest has read. The priest is reading well, clearly enough for Liza to hear him even though she is standing a long way back.

Liza listens to the familiar phrases but cannot concentrate. She is distracted by the old woman in front of her, who keeps turning round malevolently and piercing Liza with a cold stare, with a yellow-ringed eye like the eye of a fish. The old woman is afraid that Liza will singe her fox-fur collar.

Liza is also distracted by all kinds of other thoughts. She is thinking of her friend: fair, curly-headed Zina. Zina is like a bee—all honey and gold. Her bronze hair grows in tight curls. One summer, at the dacha, Zina had been sitting holding a little lapdog, and a woman coming past had said, "Humph, just look at that... poodle!" And in all seriousness Zina had asked, "Was she talking about *me*, or Kadochka?" Zina is silly, and so like a bee that Liza calls her Zuzu.

What is the priest reading about now? "And the second time the cock crew."[6] How had it all happened? Night. A fire in the courtyard of the high priest. It must have been cold. People were keeping warm next to the fire. And Peter was sitting with them. Liza loved Peter; for her he always had a special place among the apostles. She loved him because he was the most passionate of them. She didn't like to think that Peter had denied Christ. When they had asked him if he had been with Jesus of Nazareth, and he had not admitted it, it was only because he didn't want to be driven away. After all, he had followed Christ into the high priest's courtyard—he had not been afraid then.

Liza thinks of how Peter wept and of how he walked away "the second time the cock crew", and her heart aches, and, in her soul, she walks side by side with Peter, past the guards, past the terrible, cruel soldiers, past the high priest's servants, who look on with malevolent suspicion, and out through the gate and into the black, grief-stricken night.

And so the night goes on. From the square outside Pontius Pilate's house comes the hubbub of the crowd. And just then a voice, loud and forceful as fate itself, cries out, "Crucify Him! Crucify Him!" And it seems as if the flames of the candles shiver, and an evil black breath spreads through the church: "Crucify Him! Crucify Him!" And from age to age it has been passed down, that evil cry. What can we do, how can we make amends, how can we silence that cry, so that we no longer need hear it?

Liza feels her hands grow cold; she feels her whole body transfixed in a sort of ecstasy of sadness, with tears running down her cheeks. "What is it? Why am I crying? What's the matter with me?"

"Perhaps I should tell Zuzu," she thinks. "But how can I make Zuzu understand? Will Zuzu be able to understand how the whole church fell silent, how the flames of the candles shivered, and how that loud, terrible voice called out, 'Crucify Him! Crucify Him!'? I won't be able to tell her all that. If I don't tell it well, Zuzu won't understand anything. But if she does understand, if she feels what I feel, how wonderful, how glorious that would be. It would be something quite new. I think somehow we would start to live our whole lives differently. Dear Lord, help me be able to tell it!"

Easter Sunday was always jolly. A great many visitors would come to wish them a happy Easter. Liza had put on a spring dress made to a pattern of her own choosing. And she had chosen it because the caption beneath it in the fashion magazine read: "A dress for the young lady of thirteen". Not for a little girl, or for a growing girl, but for a young lady.

Zuzu came round for breakfast. She was looking pleased, as if she were full of secrets. "Let's go to your room. Quick. I have so much to tell you," she whispered.

The news really was extraordinary: a cadet! A divine cadet! And not a young boy, he was sixteen already. He could sing *"Tell her that my fiery soul…"*[7] Zuzu hadn't heard him, but Vera Yaroslavtseva had told her he sang very well. And he was in love with Zuzu. He had seen her at the skating rink and on Palm Sunday at Vera Yaroslavtseva's. He had seen Liza, too.

"Yes, he's seen you. I don't know where. But he said you were a magnificent woman."

"Did he really?" Liza gasped. "Did he really say that? And what does he look like?"

"I don't know for sure. When we went for a walk on Palm Sunday there were two cadets walking behind us, and I don't know which of the two he was. But I think he was the darker one, because the other one was ever so fair and round, not the sort to have strong feelings."

"And you think he's in love with *me*, too?"

"Probably. Anyway, what of it? It's even more fun if he's in love with both of us!"

"Don't you think that's immoral? It feels a little strange to me."

The bee-like Zuzu, all curls and honey, pursed her rosy lips mockingly.

"Well, I'm amazed at you, truly I am. The Queen of Sheba had all the peoples of the world in love with her—and here you are, afraid of just one cadet. That's plain silly."

"And it's really true, what he said about me? That I'm…"

Liza was embarrassed to repeat those extraordinary words ("a mag-ni-fi-cent wo-man").

"Of course it's true," said Zuzu, in a matter-of-fact way. "It's what Vera Yaroslavtseva told me. Do you think she'd make up something like that just for fun? She's probably bursting with envy."

"But all the same, don't you think it might be a sin?" Liza fretted. And then: "Wait, there's something I wanted to tell you. And now I've forgotten. Something important."

"Well, it'll come back to you. We're being called to breakfast."

In the evening, when she was going to bed, Liza went up to the mirror, looked at her fair hair, at her sharp little face with its freckled nose, smiled and whispered, "A magnificent woman."

3

The night was black.

Over to starboard, the sea flowed into the sky and it seemed that there, quite close, only a few metres from the ship, lay the end of the world. A black void, space, eternity.

Over to port, one or two little lights glimmered in the distance. They were alive, flickering, moving. Or were we just imagining this, since we all knew there was a town there? Living people, movement. Life.

After two terrible, boring weeks on board, with nobody sure where they were going and when they would arrive, or whether they would ever feel the earth beneath their feet again, or whether that earth would be kind to them or whether it would lead them to sorrow, torment and death; after that, how frustrating it was to see those living lights and not dare to sail towards them.

In the morning the captain promised to contact the shore, find out the situation there and then decide what to do.

Who was in the town? Who had control of it? Friend or foe? Whites or Reds? And if it was in enemy hands, where could we go? Farther east? But we wouldn't get far on this little coaster. We'd be drowned.[8]

Tired people wandered about on deck, looking towards the lights.

"I don't want to look at those lights," said Liza. "It makes me feel even more hopeless. I'd rather look at the black, terrible night. It feels closer to me. But isn't the sea making a strange booming sound? What is it?"

A sailor passed by.

"Can you hear?" asked Liza. "Can you hear the sea booming?"

"Yes," said the sailor, "it's church bells from the shore. That's a good sign. It means the Whites are there. Today is Holy Thursday. The Feast of the Twelve Gospels."

The Twelve Gospels. A memory comes back, from long ago. Black, gold, candlelight. The pale blue smoke of incense. A little girl with blond braids clasps her hands around a wax candle that drips and flickers. She clasps her hands and weeps, "What can we do, how can we make amends, how can we silence that cry, so that we need no longer hear it: 'Crucify Him! Crucify Him!'"

How strangely and clearly it all came back to her! So much time had passed, such a vast life, and then suddenly that moment—which, at the time, she had forgotten almost immediately—had suddenly come right up to her, in the form of church bells booming over the water, in the form of lights glowing on the shore like wax candles. It had caught up with her and now it was standing there beside her. It would never go away again. Never again? And Zuzu? Would Zuzu come running up again too, to buzz, to dance, to fly around her? The Zuzus of this world run fast, after all. They always catch up…

"And the second time the cock crew…"

1940
Translated by Rose France

The White Flower

Our friends the Zaitsevs live out of town.[1]

"The air is so much better out in the suburbs," they say. That is, they can't afford to live where the air is bad.

A small group of us went to visit them.

We set off without any mishap. That is, apart from minor details: we didn't take enough cigarettes, one of us lost her gloves, another forgot her door key. And then, at the station, we bought one ticket less than we needed. Well, anyone can make a mistake. We counted wrong. Even though there were only four of us.

It was a little awkward, actually, that we counted wrong. Apparently, in Hamburg, there was once a horse that could count beautifully, right up to six...

And we got out without any mishap at the right station. Though we did get out once or twice before—at every station, as a matter of fact. But every time, realizing our mistake, we had, very sensibly, got back in the carriage.

When we arrived at our destination we had a few more awkward moments. It turned out that none of us knew the Zaitsevs' address. Each of us was relying on the others.

A quiet, gentle voice came to our aid: "You're here!"

It was the Zaitsevs' daughter: a girl of eleven, clear-eyed, with blond Russian plaits just like I had had at that age (plaits pulled so many, many times by other children, plaits that brought me no end of grief!).

She had come to meet us.

"I really didn't think you'd get here!" she said.

"Why?"

"Well, Mama kept saying that you'd either miss the train or get the wrong one."

I was a little offended. I'm actually very punctual. Recently, when I was invited to a ball, not only did I not arrive late—I was a whole week early.

"Ah, Natasha, Natasha!" I said. "You don't know me very well yet!"

Her clear eyes looked at me thoughtfully, then down at the ground.

Delighted that we now knew where we were going, we decided to go and sit in a café for a while, then to hunt down some cigarettes, then try to telephone Paris and then…

But the fair-haired girl said very seriously, "No, you absolutely mustn't. We must go back home right away. They're expecting us."

So, shamefaced and obedient, we set off in single file behind the young girl.

We found our hostess at the stove.

She was looking bemusedly into a saucepan.

"Natasha, quick! Tell me what you think? What *is* this I've ended up with—roast beef or salt beef?"

The girl had a look.

"No, my angel," she said. "This time it looks like beef stew."

"Wonderful! Who'd have thought it?" cried Madame Zaitseva, delighted.

Dinner was a noisy affair.

We were all very fond of one another, all enjoying ourselves, and all in the mood to talk. We all talked at once. Somebody talked about the journal *Contemporary Notes*.[2] Somebody talked about how you shouldn't pray for Lenin. That would be a sin. After all, the Church didn't pray for Judas. Somebody talked about Parisian women and dresses, about Dostoevsky, about the recent spelling reform,[3] about the situation of writers abroad and about the Dukhobors,[4] and somebody wanted to tell us how the Czechs cook eggs, but she never succeeded. She kept talking away, but she was constantly interrupted.

And in all the hubbub the young girl, now wearing an apron, walked round the table, picking up a fork that had fallen onto the floor, moving a glass away from the edge of the table, seeing to all our needs, taking our worries to heart, her blond plaits glinting as bright as ever.

At one point she came up to one of us and held out a ticket.

"Look," she said. "I want to show you something. In your own home, is it you who looks after the housekeeping? Well, when you next buy some wine, ask for one of these tickets. When you've collected a hundred tickets, they'll give you six towels."

She kept pointing things out to us and explaining things. She very much wanted to help—to help us live in the world.

"How wonderful it is here," enthused our hostess. "After the lives we led under the Bolsheviks! It's barely believable. You turn on a tap—and water comes out. You go to light the stove—and there's firewood already there."

"Eat up, my angel," the girl whispered. "Your food will go cold."

We talked until it grew dark. The fair-haired girl had for some time been repeating something to each of us in turn. At last somebody paid attention.

"You need to catch the seven o'clock train," she had been saying. "You must go to the station straight away."

We grabbed our things and ran to the station.

There we had one last, hurried conversation.

"We need to buy Madame Zaitseva a dress tomorrow. Very modest, but showy. Black, but not too black. Narrow, but it must look full. And most important of all, one she won't grow tired of."

"Let's take Natasha with us. She can advise us."

And off we went again: *Contemporary Notes*, Gorky, French literature, Rome…

And the fair-haired girl was walking about, saying something, trying to convince us of something. At last, somebody listened.

"You need to go over the bridge to the other platform. Don't wait till the train comes in or you'll have to rush and you might miss it."

The next day, in the shop, the graceful figure of Madame Zaitseva was reflected in two triple mirrors. A little salesgirl with pomaded hair and short legs was draping one dress after another over her. And on a chair, her hands politely folded, sat the fair-haired girl, dispensing advice.

"Oh!" said Madame Zaitseva, flitting about between the mirrors. "This one is lovely. Natasha, why aren't you giving me any advice? Look, isn't that beautiful—with the grey embroidery on the front. Quick, tell me what you think!"

"No, my angel, you mustn't buy a dress like that. How could you go about every day with a grey stomach? It would be different if you had a lot of dresses. But as it is, it's not very practical."

"Well, fancy you saying that!" her mother protested. But she didn't dare disobey.

We began to make our way out.

"Oh!" cried Madame Zaitseva, "Just look at these collars! They're just what I've been dreaming of! Natasha, take me away from them quickly, don't let me get carried away!"

Concerned, the fair-haired girl took her mother by the hand.

"Come this way, my angel, don't look over there. Come over here and look at the needles and thread."

"You know what?" whispered Madame Zaitseva, with a sideways glance at her daughter. "She heard what we were saying about Lenin yesterday. And in the evening she said, 'I pray for him every day. People say he has much blood on his conscience. It's a burden on his soul... I can't help it,' she said to me, 'I pray for him.'"[5]

1924
Translated by Rose France

PART III

Heady Days: Revolutions and Civil War

New Life

It was not long after the war with Japan.[1] Forty-five years ago. An extraordinary time, and it comes back to me in bits and pieces, as if somebody had shuffled the pages of a diary, mixing up the tragic entries with stories so ridiculous that one can only shrug in disbelief. Did all that really happen? Was life really like that? Were other people, were we ourselves, really like that?

But yes, that is exactly how it was.

Russia had swung to the left overnight. There was unrest among the students, there were strikes among the workers, and even old generals could be heard snorting about the disgraceful way the country was being run, and making sharp criticisms of the Tsar himself.

Sometimes all this became the stuff of farce. In Saratov, the Chief of Police joined up with Topuridze—a revolutionary who had just married a millionairess—to publish a legally authorized Marxist newspaper.[2] Things could hardly have got more absurd.

The Petersburg intelligentsia took keen delight in the new political climate. One of our theatres put on *The Green Cockatoo*[3]– a previously censored play about the French Revolution. Journalists wrote satirical pieces undermining the establishment, poets wrote revolutionary verses and actors declaimed them on stage to enthusiastic applause.

The university and the technological institute were temporarily closed, and political meetings took place in their buildings. Ordinary, respectable city folk would wander quite freely into these meetings, draw inspiration from the shouts of "Hear, hear!" and "Down with this! Down with that!"—still a novelty at the time—and take any number of half-baked, badly formulated ideas back home to their friends and families.

New illustrated journals appeared: one, edited by Shebuev, was called the *Machine Gun*.[4] The cover of one issue, if I remember correctly, was adorned by a bloody handprint. These publications took the place of the respectable *Wheatfield*[5] and sold out quickly, bought eagerly by a rather surprising readership.

I remember once, at my mother's house, meeting one of her old friends, the widow of an important dignitary. This dignitary had been a friend of Katkov and a diehard conservative of the type we later came to call "bison".[6]

"I should like to read the *Machine Gun*," said this dignitary's widow, for some reason pronouncing the dreadful word not with a "u" but with a clipped "e": "Machine G*e*n". "But I don't dare buy it myself, and I don't like to send Yegor out to get it. I feel Yegor doesn't approve of the latest tendencies."

Yegor was her old manservant.

There was also an occasion when my uncle and I were at my mother's. This uncle had been close to the royal court and, when we were children, he had often brought us sweets from the Tsar's table (which was quite the done thing back then). The sweets were made by the Tsar's own confectioner, and were in white wrappers with trimmed edges. We had chewed on them with awe. Now, pointing at me, my mother said to my uncle, "*This* young lady mixes with socialists."

It was as if she were talking about some savage she had seen devouring a raw partridge, feathers and all. Something rather revolting—yet still impressive.

"Now there'll be trouble," I thought.

But to my surprise, there was nothing of the kind.

My uncle smiled archly: "Well, my dear," he said, "young people must move with the times."

This was the last thing I had expected.

So how was it I began to move with the times?

In our circle of friends there was a certain K.P.,[7] the son of a senator. Much to his father's chagrin, he was closely involved with the Social Democrats.[8] He was a restless soul, torn between Lenin's pamphlet "One Step Forward, Two Steps Back"[9] and the poems of Balmont.

"You really must go and see Lenin in Geneva,"[10] he would say to me.

"Why Lenin? Why should I go and see Lenin?"

"Why? To study with him. That's just what you need."

At that point I had only just started to publish my work. My articles and sketches were being published in the *Stock Exchange Gazette*,[11] a paper devoted mainly to castigating the city fathers—those who had managed to grab for themselves a piece of the public "pie". I was contributing to this castigation. One of the popular topics of the day was a plan by the city governor, Lelyanov, to fill in the Catherine Canal.[12] I had written a verse fable entitled "Lelyanov and the Canal":

One day Lelyanov, on his morning stroll,
Clapped eyes upon the Catherine Canal,
And said, a frown upon his face,
"You really are a waste of space
Not even a canal, just a disgrace!
No one can swim in you, or sail or drink your water
In short, you just don't do a thing you ought to.
I'll fill you in, you pitiful canal.
I know I can, and so I shall!"
So thought the city chief, his brow now stern,
When out from the canal there swam a germ.
"What lunacy," it said "infects your brain?
Planner Lelyanov, better think again!"

The Tsar was against Lelyanov's plan, so he very much liked my fable. The paper's editor, Stanislav Propper, was "rewarded by a smile from his majesty", and added an extra two kopecks to my fee. In those days the only journalist who could command the legendary fee of ten kopecks was Vladimir Nemirovich-Danchenko. In short, a brilliant career lay ahead of me. What did I have to learn from Lenin?

But K.P. was not easily put off. First he introduced me to a mysterious character called Valeria Ivanovna—though I soon discovered that this was an alias. She appeared to be in her thirties, she had a tired-looking face and she wore a pince-nez. She would often ask if she could bring along some interesting acquaintance. Among those she then brought along were Lev Kamenev, Alexander Bogdanov, Martyn Mandelstam, Alexander Finn-Yenotaevsky and Alexandra Kollontai.

Her friends paid me little attention. For the most part, they talked among themselves about things like congresses, resolutions and "co-optations", of which I was entirely ignorant. They liked to repeat the phrase "iron resolve", and they liked to abuse some people they called "Mensheviks" and to quote Engels, who had argued that armed revolt on the streets of a modern city was inconceivable.[13] They were evidently on a very friendly footing with one another—they all addressed one another as "comrade".

Once they brought along an absolutely ordinary working-class man. They called him "comrade" too. Comrade Yefim. He said very little—and then, after a few visits, he disappeared. I heard somebody mention, in passing, that he had been arrested.

A few months later Yefim came back, completely transformed, in a new, pale suit and bright yellow gloves. He sat with his hands raised and his fingers spread.

"Why are you doing that?" I asked.

"I don't want to get my gloves dirty. I've been dressed as a *bourgeois*, so as not to attract attention."

It was a most unfortunate camouflage. Now his appearance was so picturesque that it was impossible not to look at him.

"So you've been in prison?" I asked. "Was it hard?"

"No, not particularly." And then, with a sudden, good-natured smile: "At Christmas they gave us roast gooses."

But I should not have been surprised by Yefim's fancy dress. Very soon, events were to convince me that it was not as silly as it had seemed to my inexperienced eye.

Valeria Ivanovna left the country for a couple of months. She came back dressed in a bright red blouse.

"Why are you got up like that?" I asked.

TEFFI

It turned out that she had entered the country on a false passport made out in the name of a sixteen-year-old girl with no education. The comrades had decided that by putting a bright red blouse on a middle-aged woman with a pince-nez and the weary face of an intellectual, they would transform her into an illiterate young teenager. And they had been right. The border guards had believed the story, and Valeria Ivanovna had arrived safely in Petersburg in her red blouse.

Later, at the time when the newspaper *New Life* was being published,[14] Lenin would hide from the police using a still more artful method. Every time he left the editorial office he would simply turn up the collar of his coat. And not once was he recognized by the agents of the secret police, even though he was, of course, under surveillance.

People began to arrive from abroad. Mainly from Switzerland. There were more of the same conversations. They all criticized the Mensheviks, and they often spoke of Plekhanov, though for some reason they always called him "Plekanov".

"Why?" I asked.

"Oh, that's how you say it in Switzerland."

Many of them would tell me proudly that Plekhanov was from an old aristocratic family. For some reason they all found this very gratifying. I had the impression that Plekhanov had got under their skin in some way, that they were very anxious to convince him of something and that they were afraid he would abandon them.

The one member of the group who stood out was Alexandra Kollontai. She was a young, very beautiful society lady, always elegantly dressed, with a coquettish habit of wrinkling her nose. I recall how she once began a speech to a women's congress with the words, "I don't know what language to use in order to make myself understood to the bourgeois women here."

And there she was on the platform, wearing a magnificent velvet dress with a mirror pendant on a golden chain that hung to her knees.

I noticed that all the comrades were very proud of Kollontai's elegance. At one point she was arrested, I don't remember exactly when or why, and the newspapers reported that she had taken fourteen pairs of shoes with her to prison. The comrades would repeat this number with reverence, lowering their voices. In exactly the same way as when they were speaking of "Plekanov's" aristocratic lineage.

Once Kollontai invited us to her house. Valeria Ivanovna led us up the back staircase. This took us straight into the kitchen, where the astonished cook asked:

"Who are you looking for?"

"We've come to see Comr... to see Kollontai."

"But what made you use the back stairs? Please go through to her study."

Valeria Ivanovna appeared to have taken it entirely for granted that comrade Kollontai's room was in the servants' quarters.

When we entered the spacious, beautifully furnished study, we were greeted by Kollontai's friend, Finn-Yenotaevsky, a tall dark man with a pointed face and hair like a bush of Austrian broom. Each of the curly dark hairs on his head grew in a distinct spiral, and one half-expected these spirals to chime together in the wind.

We were served tea and biscuits, just as you might expect in any well-to-do household, but then it was back to the same old conversations: the Mensheviks... as Engels said... iron resolve... Plekanov... Plekanov... Plekanov... Mensheviks... co-optation.

It was all extraordinarily dull. They were always picking over some trivial bone of contention: perhaps someone had been abroad and brought back some senseless Party gossip; or someone had drawn caricatures of the Mensheviks, which provoked childish amusement among the bearded Marxists with their "iron resolve". And all the while, hardened agents provocateurs, whose role only came to light many years later, were strolling about happily in their midst.[15]

They talked about how the Mensheviks were accusing Lenin of having "pocketed ten francs intended for Menshevik use" ("pocketed"—that was the word the Mensheviks were using). Abroad, the Mensheviks were interrupting speeches by the Bolsheviks, caterwauling when Lunacharsky appeared in public, and had even tried to run off with a cash box full of admission money, which the Bolsheviks had defended with their fists.

All these conversations were of no interest to anyone not directly involved, and did nothing to inspire respect. There was no talk of Russia's fate—of her past or future. These people seemed entirely unconcerned by everything that had aroused the indignation of earlier generations of revolutionaries; they had no interest in the principles for which earlier generations had been willing to pay with their lives. Life simply passed them by. Often some important event, a strike in a big factory or some other major disturbance, would take them completely unawares. They would quickly send *their men* to the scene, but of course, their men would arrive too late. In this way they failed to anticipate the importance of Father Gapon's movement,[16] and remained blind to much else besides—failures that would later be a source of embarrassment to them.

Real life held no interest for these people. They were up to their ears in their congresses, co-optations and resolutions.

But there was one thoroughly bourgeois character, Pyotr Rumyantsev. Cheerful, witty, a ladies' man and a lover of good food, he often went to the "Vienna" literary restaurant and liked to tell amusing stories about his comrades. How he fitted in among these other comrades was hard to understand; it was equally hard to believe in his iron resolve.

"One of our ships has sunk with a cargo of arms," he would announce cheerfully. "Bad news, I'm afraid." Then he would add with a sigh, "Let's go and have a good breakfast at the 'Vienna'. The workers' movement still needs our strength."

What could we do? If our strength was still needed, then we needed to keep it up. Far be it from us to shirk our civic responsibilities.

Finn-Yenotaevsky was someone I saw only occasionally. But once he appeared unexpectedly with some strange news.

"Tomorrow there will be a mass demonstration by the proletariat. We're setting up a first-aid station in the editorial office of *Life Questions*[17] on Saperny Lane. There will be a medical orderly there, and materials for bandaging the dead and wounded."

I was somewhat taken aback. Why were they planning to bandage the dead?

But Finn-Yenotaevsky saw nothing odd about any of this. He fumbled in his wallet and pulled out ten roubles.

"This is for your expenses. Be at the first-aid station at three o'clock sharp. In addition, I'd like you to go to Liteyny Street, to house number five, and tell Dr Prunkin that he must be in

Saperny Lane, in the editorial office of *Life Questions*, at three o'clock sharp, without fail. Don't forget now, and don't mix anything up. Prunkin, Liteyny, ten—I mean, five. Prunkin Street."

"And what did you say the ten roubles are for?"

"For expenses."

"And will K.P. be there too?"

"He should be. So don't forget, don't mix anything up. And be punctual. We need discipline, my friends, or everything will be ruined! So. Five o'clock sharp—to Dr Liteyny. Don't write anything down. You need to remember it."

And he dashed off, his spirals chiming.

I knew the editorial staff of *Life Questions* and had even been invited to work on the paper. As far as I remember, the editors were Nikolai Berdyaev and Sergei Bulgakov (Father Sergius as he later became). Our friend Georgy Chulkov was the secretary and Alexei Remizov was the business manager. Remizov's wife, Serafima Pavlovna, proofread the manuscripts. In short, they were people I knew. I remember Berdyaev once saying to me, "So you're keeping company with the Bolsheviks, are you? I'd advise you to stay away from them. I know that crowd. We were in exile together. I wouldn't have any dealings with them if I were you."

As I was not exactly having "dealings" with them, Berdyaev's warning had not bothered me.

Now, however, an undeniably Bolshevik first-aid station was to be set up in Berdyaev's editorial office. If it was being organized by Finn-Yenotaevsky, there was no doubt about its Bolshevik credentials. Or was Finn-Yenotaevsky merely acting in the capacity of a member of some medical committee for the bandaging of dead people? I was reassured by the thought that K.P. would be there. He would explain everything to me. It was all a little strange, of course, but there was no going back now. I had ten roubles in my hand and an important mission to carry out. I had to act.

I went to Liteyny Street.

But it turned out that there was no doctor to be found—neither at number five, nor at number ten. I made enquiries, thinking there might be a doctor who wasn't called Prunkin. Or a Prunkin who wasn't a doctor. But there was no one at all. No doctor—and no Prunkin. I returned home quite dismayed.

For the first time in my life, the proletariat had entrusted me with an important mission, and I had achieved nothing. If my aristocratic elders and betters ever found out, they would look on me with scorn. Only one thing reassured me—my old friend K.P. would be at the first-aid station too. He would protect me.

The following morning I listened out carefully—was there any shooting to be heard? No, there was nothing. It was all quiet. At three o'clock sharp ("Discipline, my friends, above all!") I entered the building. At the door of the editorial office I ran into K.P.

"Well?" I asked.

He shrugged.

"Nothing. Nothing and nobody."

A girl came in, carrying a packet of hygroscopic cotton wool. She sat there for five minutes and then went away again, taking the cotton wool with her.

The next day, Finn-Yenotaevsky appeared.

"You know," I said, "I couldn't find any doctor at all on Liteyny Street, either at number five or at number ten."

"You couldn't?" he said, without the least surprise. "Well, you won't help us bring about the revolution. Give me back the ten roubles."

"So, if I had found a doctor, you'd have brought about a revolution?"

But he just gave a toss of his spirals and dashed off.

"I'm sick of all your friends," I said to K.P. "Can't we put them off somehow?"

"Wait a little longer," he replied. "Lenin will be here soon. Only don't tell a soul. He's coming illegally. Once he's here, things will get interesting. Do please wait a little."

And so I began waiting for Lenin.

Maxim Gorky came to me with a request.

He told me he often received communications from the provinces, which were of interest only to himself and his friends, and of no interest whatsoever to anybody else. At that time, anyone receiving too much correspondence was liable to attract the attentions of the police, and then their letters would be intercepted and begin to go missing. However, if the correspondence was sent to an editorial office, it wouldn't attract any attention at all. The head of the provincial affairs desk at the *Stock Exchange Gazette* was a man of very liberal views by the name of Linyov.[18] I was to ask Linyov for a favour: not to print any letters he received from the provinces in which the date was underlined twice. Apparently, the contents of these letters (which were quite innocuous and, actually, pure fabrication) were intended only for Gorky and his friends. Instead of printing the letters, Linyov was to pass them to me, as I often came in to the editorial office. And then Gorky's friends would pick them up from me.

It was all quite clear and simple.

Linyov was happy to oblige.

This Linyov was a man who didn't do things by halves. He had an extravagant head of hair and a beard that seemed to ripple in the breeze.

"I appeal to Gogol's Russia, to Dostoevsky's Russia. I ask them 'Where are we heading?'" he would say. "But I get no answer."

It was too bad that he got no answer from either Gogol's or Dostoevsky's Russia, but he took no offence, and went on repeating his impossible question.

Anyway, Linyov agreed, and even gave his word that he would always do everything he possibly could to help Gorky's friends. Presently, Linyov passed me two or three letters with the dates underlined. A gentleman who claimed to be "from Gorky" came and took them away. The letters seemed to be utterly trivial: "Students at the Kursk Seminary are complaining that they have been given spoilt meat." "The Taganrog school building is in need of repair, but it is impossible to get a housing repair grant."

Then, all of a sudden, the letters stopped. The "gentleman from Gorky" arrived, very agitated. He and his friends knew that an important letter had been dispatched the week before, and that Linyov hadn't passed it on. In general, letters had started to go missing. What was going on? They had to get to the bottom of things immediately.

"Have there been any letters?" I asked Linyov.

"Of course there have," said Linyov, "As it happens, they were extremely interesting. As an experienced observer of provincial life, I simply had to print the material."

"But you were warned that it was all pure fabrication," I said. "How could you print it? Now you'll get complaints!"

"I'm already getting complaints. However, as an experienced observer… anyway, it's over now. There haven't been any more letters."

I looked into his tray. The first thing I saw was a letter with the date underlined.

"What about this?" I asked. "And here's another, and another."

"Oh, those!" His manner was blasé. "You can have them. I've used them already."

Later that day I passed on the letters to the "gentleman from Gorky". He was overjoyed and then, to my surprise, he asked for a candle. He lit the candle, and began to heat the letter over the flame.

"What are you doing?" I asked.

"What do you think I'm doing? I'm developing it."

So that was what was going on! Between the lines of the letter, yellow words began to appear. Familiar words: "co-optation", "mandate", "Mensheviks".

Three days later, Linyov rushed in. His hair was on end, his coat gaping open, and he had the face of a man who has just jumped off a cliff into the sea.

He was shouting, "I have a daughter! I may not have seen her for fifteen years, but I'm a father, I'll have you know."

"What's happened to your daughter?"

"I'll tell you what's happened to her," he said. "Her only father is about to be ruined by you and your friends. Make no mistake! Those letters! Gorky will drag me to the guillotine!"

"Don't take on so. We don't have the guillotine here. We're not in France."

"It makes no difference. You tell Gorky from me that I have a daughter!"

I promised I would pass on the message, and Linyov rushed off again, forgetting his briefcase and gloves.

I told the "gentleman from Gorky", and that was the end of the matter.

For some time now there had been talk in literary circles of the need to start a newspaper. The poet Minsky had been granted the necessary permission,[19] but he had no money. Some capitalist showed up and arranged a meeting, to which our friend K.P., who knew him, was invited. Although the plans being discussed were quite innocuous, suddenly the police burst in and arrested everybody. Nobody had done anything wrong, but the police dealt with them very harshly. Those arrested were taken to Marshal Baroch, who was well known for his bully-boy tactics. He yelled, stamped his feet and threatened to let them all rot in jail. K.P. replied, calmly, "That's fine, but I need to make a call to my father."

"Call him! Feel free!" yelled Baroch. "And I'll let him know just what sort of a son he has. He'd better watch out, too!"

In those days, you had to give the number to a switchboard operator who would put you through. When K.P. gave the girl his father's number, Marshal Baroch gave a start.

"Is that Senator P.'s apartment?" K.P. asked over the phone.

Baroch jumped to his feet.

"Igor, is that you?" continued K.P. "Could you tell father that I've been arrested and that Marshall Baroch is acting the fool?"

Marshall Baroch didn't say a word. Shamefaced, he slunk out of the room.

K.P. was released that day. The others were kept for three days.

That was the last we saw of the capitalist, and the dream of starting a newspaper was dashed.

But then fresh hope dawned. Gorky began talks with Minsky. Getting permission to start a new paper was difficult; it was easier to try to make use of the permission already granted to Minsky. Gorky found the money, and Minsky was to be the editor. The literary section would include Gorky, Zinaida Gippius (both as a poet and as a literary critic, under the pseudonym "Anton the Extreme") and myself. The paper would take its political direction from the Social Democrats, under the leadership of Lenin. Rumyantsev was to be editorial secretary and the managing editor would be Litvinov, whom we all nicknamed *Papasha* ("Daddy").

Our future secretary found a superb building on Nevsky Prospekt for our editorial office, with a grand entrance onto the street and a uniformed doorman. Everybody was very excited.

Minsky found the slogan "Workers of the World Unite" a great source of inspiration. Realizing that the phrase was pleasingly metrical, he composed an anthem:

> Workers of the world—unite!
> Ours the strength, the power, the will.
> Time to face our final fight,
> When our enemy shall fall.
> Form a chain about the globe
> Let us, chanting with one voice,
> March as one against our foe
> Till in victory we rejoice.

All our foe held in his hands
We now claim as our birthright.
We'll take the red sun for our flag.
Workers of the world—unite![20]

This anthem was printed in the first edition of the paper, which was called *New Life*.

New Life aroused a great deal of interest. The first issue went on sale at a price of three roubles. All the copies were snapped up almost immediately, that same evening. Our political directors were jubilant. They thought that they were the reason for the paper's success.

"Our comrades, the workers, have shown their support!"

Sadly, the workers had in fact remained loyal to the *Petersburg Gazette*, which was printed on a special type of paper ideal for rolling cigarettes. It was the intelligentsia, needless to say, that was interested in our new paper. They were intrigued by the novelty of a collaboration between the Social Democrats and the Decadents (Minsky and Gippius), not to mention Gorky.

Strange characters began to appear in our magnificent editorial office. They whispered in corners and exchanged meaningful looks with one another.

No one in the world of journalism knew who these people were. Even the king of Russian reporters, Lvov-Klyachko, who knew literally everyone and everything, could only look at them and shrug. It seemed that they were there at the invitation of Rumyantsev. But when we asked him who they were, he smiled slyly and said, "Wait and see."

These new people had not actually begun to work; they were merely conferring, making preparations.

And then who should turn up but my old friend Yefim, the same Yefim who, while languishing in a tsarist jail, had eaten goose for Christmas. Or, as he put it, "gooses".

Yefim, smiling bashfully, announced that he had an idea for a political article.

"So far I've only got as far as the title: 'Plehve and his Slaves'.[21] I'd like to get it printed as soon as possible."

"So where is the article?"

"Well I need a bit more time to think up the article itself."

A man by the name of Gukovsky appeared too. He opened his gap-toothed mouth wide and tapped on his gums with a fingernail. "Scurvy," he declared proudly.

From this, everyone was supposed to gather that he had spent time in exile; that he had suffered for his ideas.

We were also joined by someone called Gusev, who had just arrived from abroad. Somebody said that he "had a top-notch singing voice". All these men were more or less alike. They even spoke in the same way: curling their lips ironically and leaving their sentences unfinished.

I was asked to write something satirical for the paper.

At the time there was a lot of talk about Dmitry Trepov.[22] I no longer remember what position he held, but he was certainly someone very important; hence he was dubbed *Patron*—a name which, of course, also means "Bullet". During the suppression of a recent riot[23] he had given soldiers the order to fire and "to spare no bullet". Soon afterwards, he had been removed from his post.

The editors decided that I should mark this occasion.

I wrote a rhyme called "Bullet and the bullets":

> Trepov, you are yourself the man to blame
> For your demise; as I recall it,
> Yours were the lips from which the order came:
> "Fire away lads, spare no bullet."

My rhyme was typeset at once and was supposed to come out the following day.

But it didn't appear.

What was going on?

Some Gusev or Gukovsky popped out from one of the side rooms and explained, "I asked them to hold back your poem. I wasn't sure if it's correct to rhyme 'recall it' with 'bullet'. It will need to be discussed at an editorial meeting."

I went to see Rumyantsev.

"Pyotr Petrovich, we can't afford to delay. In a day or two, every newspaper in town will have come up with the same joke. We won't be able to print it then."

Rumyantsev ran off to the typesetters and the poem appeared the following day. And by evening, the joke about "Bullet and the bullets" was being repeated everywhere: on the streets, in trams, in clubs, in parlours, at student meetings. I would have liked to have had a word with the expert on poetry who had kept back my poem. However, all the newcomers were so like one another that I was afraid I might get the wrong man, and upset somebody entirely innocent.

"Don't bother," said Rumyantsev. "He knows anyway. He only held back your poem to show that he's an important person around here, that his word means something."

"But who is he?" I asked. "Is he a writer? How does he come to be such an expert on rhyme? And in any case, it says in the contract that 'they' are supposed to keep to the political section. If you know who did it, tell him there are one or two things I'd like to change too in their political editorials."

He laughed. "That would certainly liven up the paper," he said. "Interest has been falling off lately."

But actually, interest in the paper was not falling off.

We had had some interest from Moscow. Valery Bryusov had sent us a short story. Minsky had received a letter from Andrei Bely. The literary section was getting very lively.

There was a lot of talk at the time about new social developments, but it was difficult to detect any general trend. At salons, people discussed the government's actions. People who were themselves of low social status were saying things like: "Those workers and tradesmen are stirring things up. There's no satisfying that lot."

In the hairdresser's one day, a big, strapping woman with red cheeks, the owner of a horse cab yard, was sitting beside me having her hair set. She was saying to the hairdresser, "You know what, *Monsewer*, I'm that scared these days, I can't even leave the house."

"Why ever not?" asked the hairdresser.

"Well, everyone's saying the antilligentsia is about to cop it. It's scaring the living daylights out of me…"

In the house of a certain governor's wife I met a Baroness O. She had been brought to Russia by Zinaida Gippius.

"Why don't you have a *Carmagnole*?"[24] she was saying. "It's a lovely, cheerful revolutionary song for the triumphant people to dance to. I can write the music and one of your poets can write the words. I love writing music. I've already written two romances: one about a Turkish *pasha* in love, and the other about a queen in love. Now I can write a *Carmagnole*. So don't forget, now. Have a word with your poet friends."

In the dark corners of the editorial office there was much whispering, and the rustling of strange documents—little groups of cockroaches waving their whiskers.

Rumyantsev strode boldly about the office, like an animal-tamer in a circus. He was very pleased with all his staff, and was now waiting impatiently for Lenin's arrival, so that he could boast to him about how well he had set everything up. He was the object of disapproving whispers from the cockroaches in their corners, but he took no notice of this and only chuckled roguishly. Watching him, you would think he was merely playing at being a Bolshevik, and enjoying himself immensely. Yet he had, in his day, spent time in exile (albeit not in Siberia, but in Oryol).[25] He had translated Marx and was seen by the Bolsheviks as a powerful force in the world of literature. He barely said a word to the whisperers in the corners and sometimes even nodded in their direction and gave us a knowing wink.

But there was an odd mood in the editorial office. It was tense, unfriendly and awkward. Minsky was particularly anxious. He was the chief editor, the paper was authorized in his name, and yet he was not even being shown the political articles. Gorky was no longer coming in to the office. It seemed he had left the city.

"Wait and see," Rumyantsev tried to reassure everybody. "Soon Lenin will be here and everything will be sorted out."

I walked about the office, quietly singing, "The master is coming, the master will sort it all out."[26]

Rumyantsev was right.

The master did come.

And he did sort it all out.

Sitting in reception were Rumyantsev and two other men. One of them I recognized as one of our whisperers, but the other was new to me. The new man was plain and rather plump with a large lower jaw, a prominent forehead with thinning hair, small, crafty eyes and jutting cheekbones. He was sitting with one leg crossed over the other, explaining something to Rumyantsev very emphatically. Rumyantsev kept spreading his hands in dismay and shrugging his shoulders. He was clearly put out.

The whisperer was devouring this newcomer with his eyes, nodding at his every word and even bobbing up and down impatiently on his chair.

When I came in, the conversation immediately broke off. Rumyantsev introduced me and the newcomer said amiably, "Yes, yes, I know" (not that there was really much to know).

Rumyantsev did not tell me the man's name. Clearly I was expected to know already.

"Vladimir Ilyich is unhappy with our premises," said Rumyantsev.

Ah! Vladimir Ilyich! The man himself!

"The premises are excellent," Lenin interrupted. "But not for our editorial office. What on earth gave you the idea of having our office on Nevsky Prospekt? And to have such a grand doorman on duty! No ordinary working man would have the courage to walk past a figure like him. And your diarists are no use at all. You must have diaries written by workers…"

"It's anyone's guess what they'd come up with," Rumyantsev said crossly.

"It doesn't matter. Of course it will be badly written and incoherent, but that isn't important. We can take a piece, work on it, correct it and publish it. And then the workers will know it's their paper."

I thought of Yefim and his "Plehve and his Slaves".

"And will the workers be writing the literary reviews and the theatre and opera reviews, too?" I asked.

"Nowadays we don't need theatre. Nor do we need music. We don't need any articles about art or culture of any sort. The only way we can connect with the masses is by publishing diaries written by workers. Your much-touted Lvov gives us nothing but ministerial gossip. He is quite surplus to requirements."

Poor Rumyantsev. He had been so proud to have lured Klyachko-Lvov, the king of reporters, to his paper.

Klyachko was an extraordinary reporter. His exploits were legendary. Once, apparently, he had sat under the table in the office of the Home Secretary during a closed meeting. The next day, an account of this meeting appeared in Klyachko's paper in the section called "Rumours". It caused panic among those at the top. How could the reporter have found all this out? Who had let the information slip? Or had a bribe of several thousand changed hands? But then, that was a monstrous suggestion! For some time, people tried to identify the guilty party—and they, of course, got nowhere. The guilty party was the footman, who had received a hefty tip from Klyachko for hiding him under the green baize.

According to another story, Klyachko had once interviewed a certain dignitary who was preparing an important state project. The man refused to tell Klyachko anything at all definite. He restricted himself to very general comments, all the time stroking a manuscript that lay in front of him on the table. The dignitary was in a hurry to get to a meeting and Klyachko obligingly offered to take him there. As he was leaving, Klyachko suddenly realized he had left his briefcase behind in the office. The dignitary was already seated in the carriage, and Klyachko had his foot on the step when, with a sudden start, he said, "My briefcase! Goodness! I've left my briefcase behind!"

And off he dashed, back into the house.

In full view of the startled doorman, he burst into the study, and grabbed not only his briefcase but also the manuscript that was lying on the table.

An hour later, after he had had a quick look through the manuscript, he went back to the statesman's house and said to the doorman, "Your master said I was to put these papers on his table myself."

The next day the statesman was astonished to see a general outline of his project in the papers: "I gave very evasive answers to all that reporter's questions. He must have the most extraordinary nose for a story."

And Lenin was proposing to dismiss this king of reporters, Klyachko-Lvov, sought after by every paper. To replace him with what? With Yefim and his Plehves and Slaves.

"Might I ask?" I said to Lenin. "Is the entire literary section surplus to requirements, in your opinion?"

"Speaking quite frankly, yes. But wait a bit. Carry on as you are, and we'll soon reorganize everything."

The reorganization began at once. It began with the premises. Carpenters appeared, carrying lengths of wood, and began to divide each room into several compartments.

The result was a cross between a beehive and a menagerie: a maze of dark corners, cages and stables. Some cubicles were the size of stalls meant for a single horse, while others were still more cramped, like cages for smaller animals—foxes, for instance. And the partitions were so close that, had there been bars, visitors might have poked the animals with their umbrellas, or perhaps even plucked up the courage to stroke them. In some of these cubicles there was neither a desk nor a chair, only a bare light bulb on a wire.

A great number of new people appeared. All of them unknown to us and all of them alike. The ones who stood out were Martyn Mandelstam, who was interesting and intelligent, Alexander Bogdanov, who was a little dull but generally highly thought of, and Lev Kamenev who was fond of literature, or who, at any rate, acknowledged its right to exist. But these men hardly ever came into the editorial office; they were, I think, exclusively occupied with Party business. All the others would congregate in little groups in the stables with their heads facing one another, like sheep in a snowstorm. At the centre of every group there was always a piece of paper held in somebody's hand. Everybody would be stabbing at it with their fingers and muttering under their breath. Either they were struggling to get to the bottom of something, or they were all keeping tabs on one another.

A strange office indeed.

The only room untouched was the large room used for editorial meetings.

The way these meetings were conducted was also somewhat absurd. People who had nothing to do with the newspaper would come along and stand between the chairs and the wall, shrugging their shoulders and making ironical long faces, even when the question under discussion was perfectly simple and there was nothing to be ironical about: should we, for instance, print the names of deceased people in small print, or in regular type?

At one of these meetings we were told that a certain Faresov (a Populist, apparently) had just appeared. He would like to work for the newspaper.

"Anyone have any objections to Faresov?" asked Lenin.

Nobody did.

"Well, I can't say I like him myself," I said. "But that, of course, is neither here nor there."

"I see," said Lenin. "Well, since Nadezhda Alexandrovna doesn't like him for some reason, I suggest we forget about him. Tell him we're busy now."

My goodness, what a gentleman! Who would have thought it?

"See how important your opinion is to him!" K.P said to me in a whisper.

"I think this is just an excuse to get rid of Faresov," I said.

Lenin, who was sitting next to me, squinted at me out of his narrow, crafty eyes and laughed.

Meanwhile, life in the city went on as usual.

Young journalists courted young female revolutionaries who had just returned from abroad.

There was one woman (I think she was called Gradusova, though I don't remember for sure) who carried grenades around in her muff. The staff of the bourgeois *Stock Exchange Gazette* were captivated by her.

"She dresses elegantly, she goes to the hairdresser, and all the time she's carrying bombs wrapped up in her muff. Well, say what you like, but she's certainly an original! And always so calm and natural, with a smile on her face—she's an absolute darling!"

There were collections to raise money for weapons.

Absolute and original darlings like this Gradusova made the rounds of newspaper offices and high-class theatres asking coquettishly for donations towards the purchase of weapons.

One rich actress reacted to an appeal of this sort in a very businesslike fashion. She donated twenty roubles, but asked for a receipt: "If revolutionaries come to rob my apartment, I can show them I did my bit for their cause. Then they'll leave me in peace."

Gusev came to see me, but I refused to collect money myself. I have no understanding of that sort of thing and no idea how to go about it. It so happened that an English journalist from *The Times* was visiting me just then. This journalist laughed, and gave Gusev a ten-rouble gold coin. Gusev put the loot in a large paper bag which had once held biscuits from the Chuev Bakers. So far he'd collected a grand total of three one-rouble notes and a twenty kopeck coin.

Not long after this, I had another amusing encounter with this same Gusev.

My bourgeois friends took me out one evening for an after-theatre dinner, in an expensive restaurant with music and a cabaret. The clientele was wealthy—everyone was drinking champagne.

And suddenly, not far away from us, I saw a young girl who looked completely out of place there. Her face was covered in thick white make-up and she was gaudily dressed—she could have been Sonia Marmeladova on her way back from the Haymarket.[27] And next to her, behind a silver ice bucket with a bottle of champagne in it, I caught a glimpse of a familiar face. It peeped out for a moment, then disappeared. I didn't even manage to make out who it was, but one of my companions said, "There's a man over there who's very interested in you. Third table along. He keeps sneaking looks at you."

I turned round suddenly and found myself looking right at Gusev. It was he who'd been hiding from me behind the bottle. He tried to hide again but, realizing that I had spotted him, decided to take the initiative. He came over to our table, red in the face, perspiring and embarrassed: "You see, this is the sort of den of iniquity I have to hide out in from time to time…"

"You poor thing," I sighed. "I understand you only too well. *We've* all taken the decision to hide out here, too. To think what we're forced to endure. Music, ballet, Neapolitan songs. It's unbearable."

He blushed an even deeper red, made a snuffling noise, and left.

A piece of literary criticism by "Anton the Extreme" (Zinaida Gippius) was not published. And a review of a new play also failed to appear.

Why?

"Lenin says it's of no interest to the working-class reader," we were told. "The working-class reader has no interest in literature and does not go to the theatre."

I asked Lenin about this.

"Yes," he said. "That's right. Now is not the time."

"But workers aren't the only readers of our paper."

"Maybe so, but they're the only readers we're interested in."

"But don't you think that, if you get rid of the entire literature section, the paper will lose a lot of subscribers? And then you'll lose money. Anyway, if you turn the paper into some Party rag, you'll be shut down before you know it. So long as big literary names continue to appear, the censors won't look at the paper too closely: these literary names are your camouflage. But if you lose them, everybody will be able to see that the paper is simply a Party rag: you'll be shut down in no time."

"It doesn't matter," said Lenin. "If this scheme fails, we'll just think up something else."

"I see—so no theatre, then, and no music!"

Meanwhile Gukovsky, who was also present, kept nodding his agreement with Lenin.

I went to talk to Rumyantsev.

"Pyotr Petrovich," I said, "your paper will be shut down."

"Well you must try and get him to see sense. After all, we have responsibilities to our literary staff. We have a contract. The official authorization for the paper is in Minsky's name. We can't oust Minsky from the editorial committee. There'd be the most appalling literary scandal."

As I was coming out of the editorial office, I saw Gukovsky. He was going through the post.

"Excellent," he said. "Tickets for the opera. My wife adores music. We'll definitely go."

I stopped him. "No no, my friend, you won't be going any-where. That would be absolutely incompatible with the iron resolve now required of you. If there are no theatre reviews in the paper, the staff have no right to enjoy free theatre tickets. You did, after all, agree with Vladimir Ilyich just now when he said that we don't need music or literature any more. You've got to be more consistent. So—what you and I must jointly do is to take these vile inducements to unprincipled time-wasting and simply tear them up."

I put the tickets one on top of the other and calmly ripped them in half and then in half again. Only half an hour later, needless to say, I felt cross with myself for treating him so meanly. Why shouldn't the man have gone to the opera with his wife to see *Eugene Onegin*? It might have done him good. Of course he was in awe of Lenin. Of course he was afraid of Lenin and felt he had to agree with Lenin's every word—but he was still a human being! He wanted to listen to music. And he loved his wife. Why had I been so spiteful? Really I should get him some tickets and send them to him anonymously, with a little note: "I hear you're fond of music." But no, that would only scare him: he would wonder what was going on and what people were saying about him. A man like him should, of course, have nothing whatever to do with the opera! That wouldn't be a Bolshevik step forward—it would be two whole steps back..."[28] Still, all in all, the episode left a bad taste in my mouth. If they sent us any more tickets, I thought, I would definitely slip them into Gukovsky's stable.

Lenin was living in Petersburg illegally. He was, of course, under official surveillance. There was no doubt about that. Nevertheless, he would come into the office, quite freely, day after day, simply turning up the collar of his coat when he left so as not to be recognized. And not one of the gumshoes on duty ever asked any questions about this character who was so keen to cover up his chin.

The mood of those days was bucolic; the lion lay down with the lamb.

When I became aware of the relationship between Lenin and his fellow Party-members, I began to pay closer attention to him.

His appearance was unprepossessing. Slightly balding, rather short, untidily dressed, he could have been a minor official from some remote local council. There was nothing about him to suggest a future dictator. There was no suggestion of passionate fervour. He spoke and gave orders just as if he were simply going about his job like anyone else, as if he himself found it boring—but then, that was life.

He was very simple in his manner. He didn't pose. People generally pose because they want others to like them, because they yearn for beauty. Lenin had no feeling for beauty whatsoever, in anything. Lunacharsky acted the part of a "squire" and a poet. Rumyantsev fancied himself as an eagle. The whisperers were all Robespierres and Marats, even though they would all tuck their tails between their legs in the presence of Lenin.

They were all posing.

Lenin always spoke to these Marats in a friendly, good-natured way, carefully explaining anything they were slow to understand. And they would thank him warmly for enlightening them: "What on earth were we thinking of? It's so simple. Thank you!"

And in this way, acting the part of a good-natured comrade, Lenin gradually took everyone in hand and led them along his straight and narrow line—always the shortest distance between two points. And not one of these people was close or dear to him. They were no more than the material from which he pulled out threads for his own cloth.

People referred to Lenin simply as "he":

"Is he here?"

"Is he still coming? Didn't he ask you about it?"

Everybody else was "they".

He didn't single out anybody in particular. He just kept a keen watch, with his narrow, Mongolian eyes, to see who could be used, and how.

One man might be good at slipping across borders on a fake passport—he would be sent on a mission abroad. Another might be good at public speaking—he would be sent to speak at political rallies. A third was good at deciphering letters, while a fourth was good at exciting a crowd—he knew how to shout loudly and wave his arms about. And there were others who were good at putting together little articles based on the thoughts of Vladimir Ilyich.

As an orator, Lenin did not carry the crowd with him; he did not set a crowd on fire, or whip it up into a frenzy. He was not like Kerensky, who could make a crowd fall in love with him and shed tears of ecstasy; I myself witnessed such tears in the eyes of soldiers and workers as they showered Kerensky's car with flowers on Marinsky Square. Lenin simply battered away with a blunt instrument at the darkest corner of people's souls, where greed, spite and cruelty lay hidden. He would batter away and get the answer he wanted:

"Yes, we'll loot and pillage—and murder too!"

Naturally, he had no friends and no favourites. He didn't see anybody as a human being. And he had a fairly low opinion of human nature. As far as I could see, he considered everyone to be capable of treachery for the sake of personal gain. A man was good only insofar as he was necessary to the cause. And if he wasn't necessary—to hell with him. Anyone harmful or even just inconvenient could be done away with—and this would be carried out calmly and sensibly, without malice. Even amicably. Lenin didn't even seem to look on himself as a human being—he was merely a servant of a political idea. Possessed maniacs of this kind are truly terrifying.

But, as they say, history's victors are never judged. Or, as somebody once said in response to these words, "They may not be judged, but they do often get strung up without a trial."

It was rumoured that the Black Hundreds[29] from the "Tearoom of the Russian People"[30] were planning a pogrom[31] against *New Life*. Apparently they had made a list of all the paper's staff and found out their addresses. They had already decided on the night when they would do the rounds of our apartments and finish off the lot of us.

Everybody had decided not to go home that night. I had been issued with strict instructions to go somewhere else. But, as it turned out, I went to the theatre that evening, and then went on to dine with friends. I didn't get home until about five o'clock in the morning.

I decided that if the Black Hundreds were planning to kill me, they'd had all night for it —and it wasn't the kind of thing one did in the morning. I asked the doorman if anyone had called. No, no one at all. And that was that. The next day it turned out that none of the staff had had any trouble.

Nevertheless, for quite other reasons, there was a general sense of anxiety in our office.

Rumyantsev told us that Lenin was demanding we break our contract with Minsky, take over the paper entirely and make it into a Party organ. Rumyantsev thought this would be wrong and was not agreeing to it. It was Minsky who had been granted permission for the paper and it was he who was the chief editor. What on earth would the literary world think of us?

"I don't give a damn about your literary circles," said Lenin. "The thrones of tsars are toppling—and your only concern seems to be the propriety of our conduct towards a few writers."

"But it was me who signed the contract," protested Rumyantsev.

"And it'll be me who tears it up," said Lenin.

But before tearing up that ill-fated contract, he wrote an article in *New Life* that terrified us all. As far as I remember, it was something about the nationalization of land.[32] Minsky was given an official reprimand. He came into the office very shaken indeed.

"I'm the editor in chief and you tell me nothing about the articles you are including. One more article like that—and I could be sent into exile."

Minsky's wife, the poet Ludmila Vilkina, also came into the office. "I'm frightened," she said. "What if my husband does get sent to Siberia? He wouldn't survive—he has a weak chest."

In response to this entirely reasonable fear, we heard a snigger: "Oh, it's not so bad as all that in Siberia! There's a bracing climate out there in Siberia—(here there was another snigger). It's just what he needs!"

It was all very nasty. Not for one moment had Minsky imagined he would be treated like this.

It was K.P. who came to his rescue.

"Go abroad immediately," he said.

"But they might not let me out of the country."

"I'll give you my internal passport. But don't waste a moment."

A few days later, Minsky came into the office to say good-bye. He showed us the brand new external passport he had just obtained. On the English page[33] was written "gentleman" (K.P. was from a noble family).

"Look," he laughed. "Now I'm a real gentleman—with official papers to prove it."

Minsky left the country shortly after this, and the entire literary section soon resigned too. We asked for our names to be removed from the list of contributors. There was no point in us staying with the paper any longer.

Predictably enough, the paper soon closed down.

Lenin turned up the collar of his coat even farther and, still apparently unnoticed, left the country for several years.

When he came back, it was in the sealed railway carriage.[34]

1950–56
Translated by Rose France and
Robert and Elizabeth Chandler

Rasputin

There are people who are remarkable because of their talent, intelligence or public standing, people whom you often meet and whom you know well. You have an accurate sense of what these people are like, but all the same they pass through your life in a blur, as if your psychic lens can never quite focus on them, and your memory of them always remains vague. There's nothing you can say about them that everyone doesn't already know. They were tall or they were short; they were married; they were affable or arrogant, unassuming or ambitious; they lived in some place or other and they saw a lot of so-and-so. The blurred negatives of the amateur photographer. You can look all you like, but you still don't know whether you're looking at a little girl or a ram.

The person I want to talk about flashed by in a mere two brief encounters. But how firmly and vividly his character is etched into my memory, as if with a fine needle.

And this isn't simply because he was so very famous. In my life I've met many famous people, people who have truly earned their renown. Nor is it because he played such a tragic role in the fate of Russia. No. This man was unique, one of a kind, like a character out of a novel; he lived in legend, he died in legend, and his memory is cloaked in legend.

A semi-literate peasant and a counsellor to the Tsar, a hardened sinner and a man of prayer, a shape-shifter with the name of God on his lips.

They called him cunning. Was there really nothing to him but cunning?

I shall tell you about my two brief encounters with him.

I

The end of a Petersburg winter. Neurasthenia.

Rather than starting a new day, morning merely continues the grey, long-drawn-out evening of the day before.

Through the plate glass of the large bay window I can see out onto the street, where a warrant officer is teaching new recruits to poke bayonets into a scarecrow. The recruits have grey, damp-chilled faces. A despondent-looking woman with a sack stops and stares at them.

What could be more dismal?

The telephone rings.

"Who is it?"

"Rozanov."

In my surprise, I ask again. Yes, it's Rozanov.

He is very cryptic. "Has Izmailov said anything to you? Has he invited you? Have you accepted?"

"No, I haven't seen Izmailov and I don't know what you're talking about."

"So he hasn't yet spoken to you. I can't say anything over the telephone. But please, please do accept. If you don't go, I won't either."

"For heaven's sake, what are you talking about?"

"He'll explain everything. It's not something we can talk about on the telephone."

There was a click on the line. We had been disconnected.

This was all very unexpected and strange. Vasily Rozanov was not someone I saw a lot of. Nor was Izmailov. And the combination of Rozanov and Izmailov also seemed odd. What was all this about? And why wouldn't Rozanov go to some place unless I went too?

I rang the editorial department of the *Stock Exchange Gazette*, where Izmailov worked. It was too early; no one was there.

But I didn't have to wait long. About two hours later Izmailov rang me.

"There is the possibility of a very interesting meeting… Unfortunately, there's nothing more I can say over the telephone… Maybe you can guess?"

I most certainly could not guess. We agreed that he should come round and explain everything.

He arrived.

"Have you still not guessed who we're talking about?"

Izmailov was thin, all in black, and in dark glasses; he looked as if he had been sketched in black ink. His voice was hollow. All rather weird and sinister.

Izmailov truly was weird. He lived in the grounds of the Smolensk cemetery, where his father had once been a priest. He practised black magic, loved telling stories about sorcery, and he knew charms and spells. Thin, pale and black, with a thin strip of bright red mouth, he looked like a vampire.

"So you really don't understand?" he asked with a grin. "You don't know who it is we can't discuss over the telephone?"

"Kaiser Wilhelm perhaps?"

Izmailov looked through his dark glasses at the two doors into my study—and then, over his glasses, at me.

"Rasputin."

"Ah!"

"Here in Petersburg there's a publisher. Filippov—perhaps you've heard of him? No? Well, anyway, there is. Rasputin goes to see him quite often; he dines with him. For some reason he's really quite friendly with him. Filippov also regularly entertains Manuilov, who has a certain reputation in literary circles. Do you know him?"

Manuilov was someone I had come across a few times. He was one of those "companion fish" that are part of the entourage of great writers or artistic figures. At one point he had worshipped Kuprin, then he had moved over to Leonid Andreyev. Then he had quietened down and seemed to disappear altogether. Now he had resurfaced.

"This Manuilov," said Izmailov, "has suggested to Filippov that he should ask round some writers who'd like to get a glimpse of Rasputin. Just a few people, carefully chosen so there's no one superfluous and no chance of any unpleasant surprises. Only recently a friend of mine happened to be in the company of Rasputin—and someone covertly took a photograph. Worse still—they sent this photograph to a magazine. 'Rasputin,' the caption read, 'among his friends and admirers.' But my friend is a prominent public figure; he's a serious man, perfectly respectable. He can't stand Rasputin and he feels he'll never get over the disgrace of this photograph—of being immortalized amid this picturesque crowd. Which is why, to avoid any unpleasantness of this kind, I've made it a condition that there should be no superfluous guests. Filippov has given his promise, and this morning Manuilov came over and showed me the guest list. One of the writers is Rozanov, and Rozanov insists that you absolutely must be there. Without you, he says, the whole thing will be a waste of time. Evidently he has a plan of some kind."

"What on earth can this plan be?" I asked. "Maybe I should stay at home. Although I would, I admit, be curious to get a glimpse of Rasputin."

"Precisely. How could anyone not be curious? One wants to see for oneself whether he really is someone significant in his own right or whether he's just a tool—someone being exploited by clever people for their own ends. Let's take a chance and go. We won't stay long and we'll keep together. Like it or not, he's someone who'll be in the history books. If we miss this chance, we may never get another."

"Just so long as he doesn't think we're trying to get something out of him."

"I don't think he will. The host has promised not to let on that we're writers. Apparently Rasputin doesn't like writers. He's afraid of them. So no one will be telling him this little detail. This is in our interests too. We want Rasputin to feel completely at ease—as if among friends. Because if he feels he's got to start posturing, the evening will be a complete waste of time. So, we'll be going, will we? Tomorrow late—not before ten. Rasputin never turns up any earlier. If he's held up at the palace and can't come, Filippov promises to ring and let us all know."

"This is all very strange. And I've never even met the host."

"I don't know him either, not personally—nor does Rozanov. But he's someone well known. And he's a perfectly decent fellow. So, we're agreed: tomorrow at ten."

2

I had glimpsed Rasputin once before. In a train. He must have been on his way east, to visit his home village in Siberia. He was in a first-class compartment. With his entourage: a little man who was something like a secretary to him, a woman of a certain age with her daughter, and Madame V——, a lady-in-waiting to the Tsaritsa.[1]

It was very hot and the compartment doors were wide open. Rasputin was presiding over tea—with a tin teapot, dried bread rings and lumps of sugar on the side. He was wearing a pink calico smock over his trousers, wiping his forehead and neck with an embroidered towel and talking rather peevishly, with a broad Siberian accent.

"Dearie! Go and fetch us some more hot water! Hot water, I said, go and get us some. The tea's right stewed but they didn't even give us any hot water. And where is the strainer? Annushka, where've you gone and hidden the strainer? Annushka! The strainer—where is it? Oh, what a muddler you are!"

In the evening of the day Izmailov had come round—that is, the day before I was due to meet Rasputin—I went to a rather large dinner party at the home of some friends.

The mirror above the dining-room fireplace was adorned with a sign that read: "In this house we do not talk about Rasputin."

I'd seen signs like this in a number of other houses. But this time, because I was going to be seeing him the next day, there was no one in the world I wanted to talk about more than Rasputin. And so, slowly and loudly, I read out: "In this house we do not talk about Ras-pu-tin."

Sitting diagonally across from me was a thin, tense, angular lady. She quickly looked round, glanced at me, then at the sign, then back at me again. As if she wanted to say something.

"Who's that?" I asked my neighbour.

"Madame E——," he replied. "She's a lady-in-waiting. Daughter of *the* E——" He named someone then very well known. "Know who I mean?"

"Yes."

After dinner this lady sat down beside me. I knew she'd been really wanting to talk to me—ever since I'd read out that sign. But all she could do was prattle in a scatterbrained way about literature. Clearly she didn't know how to turn the conversation to the subject that interested her.

I decided to help her out.

"Have you seen the sign over the fireplace? Funny, isn't it? The Bryanchaninovs have one just like it."

She immediately came to life.

"Yes, indeed. I really don't understand. Why shouldn't we talk about Rasputin?"

"Probably because people are talking about him too much. Everyone's bored with the subject…"

"Bored?" She seemed almost scared. "How could anyone find him boring? You're not going to say that, are you? Don't you find Rasputin fascinating?"

"Have you ever met him?" I asked.

"Who? Him? You mean—Rasputin?"

And suddenly she was all fidgety and flustered. Gasping. Red blotches appeared on her thin, pale cheeks.

"Rasputin? Yes... a very little... a few times. He feels he absolutely *has* to get to know me. They say this will be very, very interesting. Do you know, when he stares at me, my heart begins to pound in the most alarming way... It's astonishing. I've seen him three times, I think, at friends'. The last time he suddenly came right up close and said, 'Why so shy, you little waif? You be sure to come and see me—yes, mind you do!' I was completely at a loss. I said I didn't know, that I couldn't... And then he put his hand on my shoulder and said, 'You shall come. Understand? Yes, you absolutely shall!' And the way he said 'shall' so commandingly, with such authority, it was as if this had already been decided on high and Rasputin was in the know. Do you understand what I mean? It was as if, to him, my fate were an open book. He sees it, he knows it. I'm sure you understand I would never call on him, but the lady whose house I met him at said I really must, that plenty of women of our station call on him, and that there's nothing in the least untoward about it. But still... I... I shan't..."

This "I shan't" she almost squealed. She looked as if she were about to give a hysterical shriek and start weeping.

I could hardly believe it! A mild-mannered lady, mousy and thin, and she looked as if she were at least thirty-five. And yet she had suddenly, shamelessly, lost all self-control at the mere mention of Rasputin, that peasant in a pink calico smock whom I had heard ordering "Annushka" to look for the tea strainer...

The lady of the house came over to where we were sitting and asked us a question. And without replying, probably without even hearing her, Madame E—— got up and with a jerky, angular gait went over to the mirror to powder her nose.

3

All the next day I was unable to put this twitching, bewitched lady-in-waiting out of my mind.

It was unnerving and horrible.

The hysteria around the name of Rasputin was making me feel a kind of moral nausea.

I realized, of course, that a lot of the talk about him was petty, foolish invention, but nonetheless I felt there was something real behind all these tales, that they sprang from some weird, genuine, living source.

In the afternoon Izmailov rang again and confirmed the invitation. He promised that Rasputin would definitely be there. And he passed on a request from Rozanov that I should wear something "a bit glamorous"—so Rasputin would think he was just talking to an ordinary "laydee" and the thought that I might be a writer wouldn't so much as enter his head.

This demand for "a bit of glamour" greatly amused me.

"Rozanov seems determined to cast me in the role of some biblical Judith or Delilah. I'll make a hash of it, I'm afraid—I haven't the talents of either an actor or an agent provocateur. All I'll do is mess things up."

"Let's just play it by ear," Izmailov said reassuringly. "Shall I send someone over to fetch you?"

I declined, as I was dining with friends, and was going to be dropped off after the meal.

That evening, as I was dressing, I tried to imagine a peasant's idea of "a bit of glamour". I put on a pair of gold shoes, and some gold rings and earrings. I'd have felt embarrassed to deck myself out any more flashily. It wasn't as if I was going to be able to explain to all and sundry that this was glamour on demand!

At my friends' dinner table, this time without any wiles on my part, the conversation turned to Rasputin. (People evidently had good reason to put injunctions up over their fireplaces.)

As always, there were stories about espionage, about Germans bribing Russian officials, about sums of money finding their way via the elder[2] into particular pockets and about court intrigues, the threads of which were all in Rasputin's hands.

Even the "black automobile" got linked with the name of Rasputin.

The "black automobile" remains a mystery to this day. Several nights running this car had roared across the Field of Mars, sped over the Palace Bridge and disappeared into the unknown. Shots had been fired from inside the car. Passers-by had been wounded.

"It's Rasputin's doing," people were saying. "Who else?"

"What's he got to do with it?"

"He profits from everything black, evil and incomprehensible. Everything that sows discord and panic. And there's nothing he can't explain to his own advantage when he needs to."

These were strange conversations. But these were strange times, and so no one was especially surprised. Although the events soon to unfold swept the "black automobile" right out of our minds. All too soon we would have other things to think about.

But at the time, at dinner, we talked about all these things. First and foremost, people were astonished by Rasputin's extraordinary brazenness. Razumov, who was then the director of the Department of Mines, indignantly related how one of his provincial officials had come to him with a request for a transfer. And to support his case, he had held out a piece of paper on which Rasputin—whom Razumov had never even met—had scrawled:

Dearie, do wot the barer asks and yul have no caws for regret.

Grigory.

"Can you imagine? The cheek of it! The brazen cheek of it! And there are a great many ministers who say they've received little notes like this. And all too many of them just do as he asks—though they don't, of course, admit as much. I've even been told I was reckless to be getting so angry, because *he* would hear about it. It was vile. Can you imagine it? 'Dearie'! As for the fine fellow who turned up with the note, I showed him what a 'Dearie' I can be! I'm told he flew down the stairs four at a time. And he had seemed like such a respectable man—as well as being a rather eminent engineer."

"Yes," said someone else, "I've heard about any number of these 'Dearie' recommendations, but this is the first time I've heard about one not being granted. People get all indignant, but they don't feel able to refuse the man. 'He's vindictive,' they say, 'a vindictive peasant.'"

4

Sometime after ten o'clock I arrived at Filippov's.

Our host greeted me in the hall. After saying in a friendly way that we'd already met once before, he showed me into his study.

"Your friends arrived some time ago."

In the small, smoke-filled room were some half a dozen people.

Rozanov was looking bored and disgruntled. Izmailov appeared strained, as if trying to make out that everything was going fine when really it wasn't.

Manuilov was standing close to the doorway, looking as if he felt entirely at home. Two or three people I didn't know were sitting silently on the divan. And then there was Rasputin. Dressed in a black woollen Russian kaftan and tall patent leather boots, he was fidgeting anxiously, squirming about in his chair. One of his shoulders kept twitching.

Lean and wiry and rather tall, he had a straggly beard and a thin face that appeared to have been gathered up into a long fleshy nose. His close-set, prickly, glittering little eyes were peering out furtively from under strands of greasy hair. I think these eyes were grey. The way they glittered, it was hard to be sure. Restless eyes. Whenever he said something, he would look round the whole group, his eyes pricking each person in turn, as if to say, "Have I given you something to think about? Are you satisfied? Have I surprised you?"

I felt at once that he was rather preoccupied, confused, even embarrassed. He was posturing.

"Yes, yes," he was saying. "I wish to go back as soon as possible, to Tobolsk. I wish to pray. My little village is a good place to pray. God hears people's prayers there."

And then he studied each of us in turn, his eyes keenly pricking each one of us from under his greasy locks.

"But here in your city nothing's right. It's not possible to pray in this city. It's very hard when you can't pray. Very hard."

And again he looked round anxiously, right into everyone's faces, right into their eyes.

We were introduced. As had been agreed, my fellow scribes did not let on who I really was.

He studied me, as if thinking, "Who *is* this woman?"

There was a general sense of both tedium and tension—not what we wanted at all. Something in Rasputin's manner—maybe his general unease, maybe his concern about the impression his words were making—suggested that somehow he knew who we were. It seemed we might have been given away. Imagining himself to be surrounded by "enemies from the press", Rasputin had assumed the posture of a man of prayer.

They say he really did have a great deal to put up with from journalists. The papers were always full of sly insinuations of every kind. After a few drinks with his cronies, Rasputin was supposed to have divulged interesting details about the personal lives of people in the very highest places. Whether this was true or just newspaper sensationalism, I don't know. But I do know that there were two levels of security around Rasputin: one set of guards whom he knew about and who protected him from attempts on his life; another set whom he was supposed not to know about and who kept track of whom he was talking to and whether or not he was saying anything he shouldn't. Just who was responsible for this second set of guards I can't say for certain, but I suspect it was someone who wanted to undermine Rasputin's credibility at court.

He had keen senses, and some animal instinct told him he was surrounded. Not knowing where the enemy lay, he was on the alert, his eyes quietly darting everywhere…

I was infected by my friends' discomfort. It felt tedious and rather awkward to be sitting in the house of a stranger and listening to Rasputin straining to come out with spiritually edifying pronouncements that interested none of us. It was as if he were being tested and was afraid of failing.

I wanted to go home.

Rozanov got to his feet. He took me aside and whispered, "We're banking on dinner. There's still a chance of him opening up. Filippov and I have agreed that you must sit beside him. And we'll be close by. You'll get him talking. He's not going to talk freely to us—he's a ladies' man. Get him to speak about the erotic. This could be really something—it's a chance we must make the most of. We could end up having a most interesting conversation."

Rozanov would happily discuss erotic matters with anyone under the sun, so it was hardly a surprise that he should be so eager to discuss them with Rasputin. After all, what didn't they say about Rasputin? He was a hypnotist and a mesmerist, at once a flagellant and a lustful satyr, both a saint and a man possessed by demons.

"All right," I said. "I'll do what I can."

Turning around, I encountered two eyes as sharp as needles. Our surreptitious conversation had obviously disturbed Rasputin.

With a twitch of the shoulder, he turned away.

We were invited to the table.

I was seated at one corner. To my left sat Rozanov and Izmailov. To my right, at the end of the table, Rasputin.

There turned out to be around a dozen other guests: an elderly lady with a self-important air ("She's the one who goes everywhere with him," someone whispered to me); a harassed-looking gentleman, who hurriedly got a beautiful young lady to sit on Rasputin's right (this young lady was dressed to the nines—certainly more than "a bit glamorous"—but the look on her face was crushed and hopeless, quite out of keeping with her attire); and at the other end of the table were some strange-looking musicians, with a guitar, an accordion and a tambourine—as if this were a village wedding.

Filippov came over to us, pouring out wine and handing round hors d'oeuvres. In a low voice I asked about the beautiful lady and the musicians.

The musicians, it turned out, were a requirement—Grisha sometimes liked to get up and dance, and only what *they* played would do. They also played at the Yusupovs'.

"They're very good. Quite unique. In a moment you'll hear for yourself." As for the beautiful lady, Filippov explained that her husband (the harassed-looking gentleman) was having a difficult time at work. It was an unpleasant and complicated situation that could only be sorted out with the help of the elder. And so this gentleman was seizing every possible opportunity to meet Rasputin, taking his wife along with him and seating her beside Rasputin in the hope that sooner or later he would take notice of her.

"He's been trying for two months now, but Grisha acts as if he doesn't even see them. He can be strange and obstinate."

Rasputin was drinking a great deal and very quickly. Suddenly he leant towards me and whispered, "Why aren't you drinking, eh? Drink. God will forgive you. Drink."

"I don't care for wine, that's why I'm not drinking."

He looked at me mistrustfully.

"Nonsense! Drink. I'm telling you: God will forgive you. He will forgive you. God will forgive you many things. Drink!"

"But I'm telling you I'd rather not. You don't want me to force myself to drink, do you?"

"What's he saying?" whispered Rozanov on my left. "Make him talk louder. Ask him again, to make him talk louder. Otherwise I can't hear."

"But it's nothing interesting. He's just trying to get me to drink."

"Get him to talk about matters erotic. God Almighty! Do you really not know how to get a man to talk?"

This was beginning to seem funny.

"Stop going on at me! What am I? An agent provocateur? Anyway, why should I go to all this trouble for you?"

I turned away from Rozanov. Rasputin's sharp, watchful eyes pricked into me.

"So you don't want to drink? You are a stubborn one! I'm telling you to drink—and you won't."

And with a quick and obviously practised movement he quietly reached up and touched my shoulder. Like a hypnotist using touch to direct the current of his will. It was as deliberate as that.

From his intent look I could see he knew exactly what he was doing. And I remembered the lady-in-waiting and her hysterical babbling: *And then he put his hand on my shoulder and said so commandingly, with such authority…*

So it was like that, was it? Evidently Grisha had a set routine. Raising my eyebrows in surprise, I glanced at him and smiled coolly.

A spasm went through his shoulder and he let out a quiet moan. Quickly and angrily he turned away from me, as if once and for all. But a moment later he was leaning towards me again.

"You may be laughing," he said, "but do you know what your eyes are saying? Your eyes are sad. Go on, you can tell me—is he making you suffer badly? Why don't you say anything? Don't you know we all love sweet tears, a woman's sweet tears. Do you understand? I know everything."

I was delighted for Rozanov. The conversation was evidently turning to matters erotic.

"What is it you know?" I asked loudly, on purpose, so that Rasputin, too, would raise his voice, as people often unwittingly do.

Once again, though, he spoke very softly.

"I know how love can make one person force another to suffer. And I know how necessary it can be to make someone suffer. But I don't want *you* to suffer. Understand?"

"I can't hear a thing!" came Rozanov's cross voice, from my left.

"Be patient!" I whispered.

Rasputin went on.

"What's that ring on your hand? What stone is it?"

"It's an amethyst."

"Well, that'll do. Hold your hand out to me under the table so no one can see. Then I'll breathe on the ring and warm it… The breath of my soul will make you feel better."

I passed him the ring.

"Oh, why did you have to take it off? That was for me to do. You don't understand…"

But I had understood only too well. Which was why I'd taken it off myself.

Covering his mouth with his napkin, he breathed onto the ring and quietly slid it onto my finger.

"There. When you come and see me, I'll tell you many things you don't know."

"But what if I don't come?" I asked, once again remembering the hysterical lady-in-waiting.

Here he was, Rasputin in his element. The mysterious voice, the intense expression, the commanding words—all this was a tried and tested method. But if so, then it was all rather naive and straightforward. Or, perhaps, his fame as a sorcerer, soothsayer and favourite of the Tsar really did kindle within people a particular blend of curiosity and fear, a keen desire to participate in this weird mystery. It was like looking through a microscope at some species of beetle. I could see the monstrous hairy legs, the giant maw—but I knew it was really just a little insect.

"Not come to me? No, you shall come. You shall come to me."

And again he quickly reached up and quietly touched my shoulder. I calmly moved aside and said, "No, I shan't."

And again a spasm went through his shoulder and he let out a low moan. Each time he sensed that his power, the current of his will, was not penetrating me and was meeting resistance, he experienced physical pain. (This was my impression at the time—and it was confirmed later.) And in this there was no pretence, as he was evidently trying to conceal both the spasms in his shoulder and his strange, low groan.

No, this was not a straightforward business at all. Howling inside him was a black beast… There was much we did not know.

5

"Ask him about Vyrubova," whispered Rozanov. "Ask him about everyone. Get him to tell you everything. And *please* get him to speak up."

Rasputin gave Rozanov a sideways look from under his greasy locks.

"What's that fellow whispering about?"

Rozanov held his glass out towards Rasputin and said, "I was wanting to clink glasses."

Izmailov held his glass out, too.

Rasputin looked at them both warily, looked away, then looked back again.

Suddenly Izmailov asked, "Tell me, have you ever tried your hand at writing?"

Who, apart from a writer, would think to ask such a question?

"Now and again," replied Rasputin without the least surprise. "Even quite a few times."

And he beckoned to a young man sitting at the other end of the table.

"Dearie! Bring me the pages with my poems that you just tapped out on that little typing machine."

"Dearie" darted off and came back with the pages.

Rasputin handed them around. Everyone reached out. There were a lot of these typed pages, enough for all of us. We began to read.

It turned out to be a prose poem, in the style of the *Song of Songs* and obscurely amorous. I can still remember the lines: "Fine and high are the mountains. But my love is higher and finer yet, because love is God."

But that seems to have been the only passage that made any sense. Everything else was just a jumble of words.

As I was reading, the author kept looking around restlessly, trying to see what impression his work was making.

"Very good," I said.

He brightened.

"Dearie! Give us a clean sheet, I'll write something for her myself."

"What's your name?" he asked.

I said.

He chewed for a long time on his pencil. Then, in a barely decipherable peasant scrawl, he wrote:

To Nadezhda
  God is lov. Now lov. God wil forgiv yu.

Grigory

The basic pattern of Rasputin's magic charms was clear enough: love, and God will forgive you.

But why should such an inoffensive maxim as this cause his ladies to collapse in fits of ecstasy? Why had that lady-in-waiting got into such a state?

This was no simple matter.

6

I studied the awkwardly scrawled letters and the signature below: "Grigory".

What power this signature held. I knew of a case where

this scrawl of seven letters had recalled a man who had been sentenced to forced labour and was already on his way to Siberia.

And it seemed likely that this same signature could, just as easily, transport a man there...

"You should hang on to that autograph," said Rozanov. "It's quite something."

It did in fact stay in my possession for a long time. In Paris, some six years ago, I found it in an old briefcase and gave it to J.W. Bienstock, the author of a book about Rasputin in French.

Rasputin really was only semi-literate; writing even a few words was hard work for him. This made me think of the forest-warden in our home village—the man whose job had been to catch poachers and supervise the spring floating of timber. I remembered the little bills he used to write: "Tren to dacha and bak fife ru" (five roubles).

Rasputin was also strikingly like this man in physical appearance. Perhaps that's why his words and general presence failed to excite the least mystical awe in me. "God is love, you *shall* come" and so on. That "fife ru", which I couldn't get out of my head, was constantly in the way...

Suddenly our host came up, looking very concerned.

"The palace is on the line."

Rasputin left the room.

The palace evidently knew exactly where Rasputin was to be found. Probably, they always did.

Taking advantage of Rasputin's absence, Rozanov began lecturing me, advising me how best to steer the conversation on to all kinds of interesting topics.

"And do please get him to talk about the Khlysts[3] and their rites. Find out whether it's all true, and if so, how it's all organized and whether it's possible, say, to attend."

"Get him to invite you, and then you can bring us along, too."

I agreed willingly. This truly would be interesting.

But Rasputin didn't come back. Our host said he had been summoned urgently to Tsarskoye Selo[4]—even though it was past midnight—but that, as he was leaving, Rasputin had asked him to tell me he would definitely be coming back.

"Don't let her go," said Filippov, repeating Rasputin's words. "Have her wait for me. I'll be back."

Needless to say no one waited. Our group, at least, left as soon as we had finished eating.

7

Everyone I told about the evening showed a quite extraordinary degree of interest. They wanted to know the elder's every word, and they wanted me to describe every detail of his appearance. Most of all, they wanted to know if they could get themselves invited to Filippov's, too.

"What kind of impression did he make on you?"

"No very strong impression," I replied. "But I can't say I liked him."

People were advising me to make the most of this connection. One never knows what the future holds in store, and Rasputin was certainly a force to be reckoned with. He toppled ministers and he shuffled courtiers as if they were a pack of cards. His displeasure was feared more than the wrath of the Tsar.

There was talk about clandestine German overtures being made via Rasputin to Alexandra Fyodorovna. With the help of prayer and hypnotic suggestion he was, apparently, directing our military strategy.

"Don't go on the offensive before such and such a date—or the Tsarevich will be taken ill."

Rasputin seemed to me to lack the steadiness needed to manage any kind of political strategy. He was too twitchy, too easily distracted, too confused in every way. Most likely he accepted bribes and got involved in plots and deals without really thinking things through or weighing up the consequences. He himself was being carried away by the very force he was trying to control. I don't know what he was like at the beginning of his trajectory, but by the time I met him, he was already adrift. He had lost himself; it was as if he were being swept away by a whirlwind, by a tornado. As if in delirium, he kept repeating the words: "God… prayer… wine". He was confused; he had no idea what he was doing. He was in torment, writhing about, throwing himself into his dancing with a despairing howl—as if to retrieve some treasure left behind in a burning house. This satanic dancing of his was something I witnessed later…

I was told he used to gather his society ladies together in a bathhouse and—"to break their pride and teach them humility"—make them bathe his feet. I don't know whether this is true, but it's not impossible. At that time, in that atmosphere of hysteria, even the most idiotic flight of fancy seemed plausible.

Was he really a mesmerist? I once spoke to someone who had seriously studied hypnotism, mesmerism and mind control.

I told him about that strange gesture of Rasputin's, the way he would quickly reach out and touch someone and how a spasm would go through his shoulder when he felt his hypnotic command was meeting resistance.

"You really don't know?" he asked in surprise. "Mesmerists always make that kind of physical contact. It's how they transmit the current of their will. And when this current is blocked, then it rebounds upon the mesmerist. The more powerful a wave the mesmerist sends out, the more powerful the current that flows back. You say he was very persistent, which suggests he was using all his strength. That's why the return current struck him with such force; that's why he was writhing and moaning. It sounds as if he was suffering real pain as he struggled to control the backlash. Everything you describe is entirely typical."

8

Three or four days after this dinner, Izmailov rang me a second time.

"Filippov is begging us to have dinner with him again. Last time Rasputin had to leave almost straight away; he'd barely had time to look about him. This time Filippov assures us that it will all be a great deal more interesting."

Apparently Manuilov had dropped in on Izmailov. He'd been very insistent (almost like some kind of impresario!) and had shown Izmailov the final guest list: all respectable people who knew how to behave. There was no need to worry.

"Just once more," Izmailov said to me. "This time our conversation with him will be a lot more fruitful. Maybe we'll get him to say something really interesting. He truly *is* someone out of the ordinary. Let's go."

I agreed.

This time I arrived later. Everyone had been at the table for some time.

There were many more people than the first time. All of the previous guests were there—as were the musicians. Rasputin was sitting in the same place. Everyone was talking politely, as if they were invited there regularly. No one was looking at Rasputin; it was as if his presence were of no consequence to them at all. And yet the truth was all too obvious: most of the guests did not know one another and, although they now seemed too timid to do anything at all, there was only one reason why they had come. They wanted to have a look at Rasputin, to find out about him, to talk to him.

Rasputin had removed his outer garment and was sitting in a stiff taffeta shirt, worn outside his trousers. It was a glaring pink, and it had an embroidered collar, buttoned on one side.

His face was tense and tired; he looked ashen. His prickly eyes were deeply sunken. He'd all but turned his back on the lawyer's glamorously dressed wife, who was again sitting next to him. My own place, on his other side, was still free.

"Ah! There she is," he said with a sudden twitch. "Well, come and sit down. I've been waiting. Why did you run off last time? I came back—and where were you? Drink! What's the matter? I'm telling you—drink! God will forgive you."

Rozanov and Izmailov were also in the same places as before.

Rasputin leant over towards me.

"I've missed you. I've been pining for you."

"Nonsense. You're just saying that to be nice," I said loudly. "Why don't you tell me something interesting instead? Is it true you organize Khlyst rituals?"

"Khlyst rituals? Here? Here in the city?"

"Well, don't you?"

"Who's told you that?" he asked uneasily. "Who? Did he say he was there himself? Did he see for himself? Or just hear rumours?"

"I'm afraid I can't remember who it was."

"You can't *remember*? My clever girl, why don't you come along and see me? I'll tell you many things you don't know. You wouldn't have English blood, would you?"

"No, I'm completely Russian."

"There's something English about your little face. I have a princess in Moscow and she has an English face, too. Yes, I'm going to drop everything and go to Moscow."

"What about Vyrubova?" I asked, rather irrelevantly—for Rozanov's sake.

"Vyrubova? No, not Vyrubova. She has a round face, not an English one. Vyrubova is my little one. I'll tell you how it is: some of my flock are little ones and some are something else. I'm not going to lie to you, this is the truth."

Suddenly Izmailov found his courage. "And... the Tsaritsa?" he asked in a choked voice. "Alexandra Fyodorovna?"

The boldness of the question rather alarmed me. But, to my surprise, Rasputin replied very calmly, "The Tsaritsa? She's ailing. Her breast ails her. I lay my hand upon her and I pray. I pray well. And my prayer always makes her better. She's ailing. I must pray for her and her little ones." And then he muttered, "It's bad... bad..."

"What's bad?"

"No, it's nothing… We must pray. They are good little ones…"

I recall reading in the newspapers, at the beginning of the revolution, about the "filthy correspondence between the elder and the depraved princesses"—correspondence that it was "quite inconceivable to publish". Sometime later, however, these letters *were* published. And they went something like this: "Dear Grisha, please pray that I'll be a good student." "Dear Grisha, I've been a good girl all week long and obeyed Papa and Mama…"

"We must pray," Rasputin went on muttering.

"Do you know Madame E——?" I asked.

"The one with the little pointed face? I think I've glimpsed her here and there. But it's you I want to come along and see me. You'll get to meet everyone and I'll tell you all about them."

"Why should I come along? It'll only make them all cross."

"Make who cross?"

"Your ladies. They don't know me; I'm a complete stranger to them. They're not going to be pleased to see me."

"They wouldn't dare!" He beat the table with his fist. "No, not in *my* house. In *my* house everyone is happy—God's grace descends on everyone. If I say, 'Bathe my feet!', they'll do as I say and then drink the water. In my house everything is godly. Obedience, grace, humility and love."

"See? They bathe your feet. No, you'll be better off without me."

"You shall come. I'll send for you."

"Has everyone really come when you've sent for them?"

"No one's refused yet."

9

Apparently quite forgotten, the lawyer's wife sitting on the other side of Rasputin was hungrily and tenaciously listening to our conversation.

From time to time, noticing me looking at her, she would give me an ingratiating smile. Her husband kept whispering to her and drinking to my health.

"You ought to invite the young lady to your right," I said to Rasputin. "She's lovely!"

Hearing my words, she looked up at me with frightened, grateful eyes. She even paled a little as she waited for his response. Rasputin glanced at her, quickly turned away and said loudly, "She's a stupid bitch!"

Everyone pretended they hadn't heard.

I turned to Rozanov.

"For the love of God," he said, "get him to talk about the Khlysts. Try again."

But I'd completely lost interest in talking to Rasputin. He seemed to be drunk. Our host kept coming up and pouring him wine, saying, "This is for you, Grisha. It's your favourite."

Rasputin kept drinking, jerking his head about, twitching and muttering something.

"I'm finding it very hard to talk to him," I said to Rozanov. "Why don't you and Izmailov try? Maybe we can all four of us have a conversation!"

"It won't work. It's a very intimate, mysterious subject. And he's shown he trusts you…"

"What's him over there whispering about?" interrupted Rasputin. "Him that writes for *New Times*?"[5]

So much for our being incognito.

"What makes you think he's a writer?" I asked. "Someone must have misinformed you... Before you know it, they'll be saying I'm a writer, too."

"I think they said you're from the *Russian Word*," he replied calmly. "But it's all the same to me."

"Who told you that?"

"I'm afraid I can't remember," he said, pointedly repeating my own words when he'd asked who had told me about the Khlysts.

He had clearly remembered my evasiveness, and now he was paying me back in kind: "I'm afraid I can't remember!"

Who had given us away? Hadn't we been promised complete anonymity? It was all very strange.

After all, it wasn't as if we'd gone out of our way to meet the elder. We had been invited. We had been offered the opportunity to meet him and, what's more, we'd been told to keep quiet about who we were because "Grisha doesn't like journalists"— because he avoids talking to them and always does all he can to keep away from them.

Now it appeared that Rasputin knew very well who we were. And not only was he not avoiding us but he was even trying to draw us into a closer acquaintance.

Who was calling the shots? Had Manuilov orchestrated all this—for reasons we didn't know? Or did the elder have some cunning scheme of his own? Or had someone just blurted out our real names by mistake?

It was all very insalubrious. What was truly going on was anyone's guess.

And what did I know about all these dinner companions of ours? Which of them was from the secret police? Which would soon be sentenced to forced labour? Which might be a German agent? And which of them had lured us here? Which member of this upright company was hoping to use us for their own ends? Was Rasputin the weaver of this web—or the one being caught in it? Who was betraying whom?

"He knows who we are," I whispered to Rozanov.

Rozanov looked at me in astonishment. He and Izmailov began whispering together.

Just then the musicians struck up. The accordion began a dance tune, the guitar twanged, the tambourine jingled. Rasputin leapt to his feet—so abruptly that he knocked his chair over. He darted off as if someone were calling to him. Once he was some way from the table (it was a large room), he suddenly began to skip and dance. He thrust a knee forward, shook his beard about and circled round and round. His face looked tense and bewildered. His movements were frenzied; he was always ahead of the music, as if unable to stop...

Everyone leapt up. They stood around him to watch. "Dearie", the one who had gone to fetch the poems, turned pale. His eyes bulged. He squatted down on his haunches and began clapping his hands. "Whoop! Whoop! Whoop! Go! Go! Go!"

And no one was laughing. They watched as if in fear and—certainly—very, very seriously.

The spectacle was so weird, so wild, that it made you want to let out a howl and hurl yourself into the circle, to leap and whirl alongside him for as long as you had the strength.

The faces all around were looking ever paler, ever more intent. There was a charge in the air, as if everyone was expecting something... Any moment!

"How can anyone still doubt it?" said Rozanov from behind me. "He's a Khlyst!"

Rasputin was now leaping about like a goat. Mouth hanging open, skin drawn tight over his cheekbones, locks of hair whipping across the sunken sockets of his eyes, he was dreadful to behold. His pink shirt was billowing out behind him like a balloon.

"Whoop! Whoop! Whoop!" went "Dearie", continuing to clap.

All of a sudden Rasputin stopped. Just like that. And the music broke off, as if that is what the musicians had intended all along.

Rasputin collapsed into an armchair and looked all around. His eyes were no longer pricking people; they seemed vacant, bewildered.

"Dearie" hastily gave him a glass of wine. I went through into the drawing room and told Izmailov I wanted to leave.

"Sit down for a moment and get your breath back," Izmailov replied.

The air was stifling. It was making my heart pound and my hands tremble.

"No," said Izmailov. "It's not hot in here. It's just your nerves."

"Please, don't go," begged Rozanov. "Now you can get him to invite you to one of his rituals. There'll be no difficulty now!"

By now most of the guests had come through and were sitting around the edges of the room, as if in anticipation of some sort of performance. The beautiful woman came in, too, her husband holding her by the arm. She was walking with her head bowed; I thought she was weeping.

I stood up.

"Don't go," said Rozanov.

I shook my head and went out towards the hall. Out of the dining room came Rasputin. Blocking my path, he took my elbow.

"Wait a moment and let me tell you something. And mind you listen well. You see how many people there are all around us? A lot of people, right? A lot of people—and no one at all. Just me and you—and no one else. There isn't anyone else standing here, just me and you. And I'm saying to you: come to me! I'm pining for you to come. I'm pining so badly I could throw myself down on the ground before you!"

His shoulder went into spasms and he let out a moan.

And it was all so ludicrous, both the way we were standing in the middle of the room together and the painfully serious way he was speaking...

I had to do something to lighten the atmosphere.

Rozanov came up to us. Pretending he was just passing by, he pricked up his ears. I started to laugh. Pointing at him, I said to Rasputin, "But he won't let me."

"Don't you listen to that degenerate—you come along. And don't bring him with you, we can do without him. Rasputin may only be a peasant, but don't you turn up your nose at him. For them I love I build stone palaces. Haven't you heard?"

"No," I replied, "I haven't."

"You're lying, my clever girl, you *have* heard. I can build stone palaces. You'll see. I can do many things. But for the love of God, just come to me, the sooner the better. We'll pray together. Why wait? You see, everyone wants to kill me. As soon as I step outside, I look all around me: where are they, where are their ugly mugs? Yes, they want to kill me. Well, so what! The fools don't understand who I am. A sorcerer? Maybe I am. They burn sorcerers, so let them burn me. But there's one thing they don't understand: if they kill me, it will be the end of Russia. Remember, my clever girl: if they kill Rasputin, it will be the end of Russia. They'll bury us together."

He stood there in the middle of the room, thin and black—a gnarled tree, withered and scorched.

"And it will be the end of Russia… the end of Russia…"

With his trembling hand crooked upwards, he looked like Chaliapin singing the role of the miller in Dvořák's *Rusalka*. At this moment he appeared dreadful and completely mad.

"Ah? Are you going? Well if you're going, then go. But just you remember… Remember."

As we made our way back from Filippov's, Rozanov said that I really ought to go and visit Rasputin: if I refused an invitation coveted by so many, he would almost certainly find it suspicious.

"We'll all go there together," he assured me, "and we'll leave together."

I replied that there was something in the atmosphere around Rasputin I found deeply revolting. The grovelling, the collective hysteria—and at the same time the machinations of something dark, something very dark and beyond our knowledge. One could get sucked into this filthy mire—and never be able to climb out of it. It was revolting and joyless, and the revulsion I felt entirely negated any interest I might have in these people's "weird mysteries".

The pitiful, distressed face of the young woman who was being thrust so shamelessly by her lawyer husband at a drunken peasant—it was the stuff of nightmares, I was seeing it in my dreams. But he must have had many such women—women about whom he shouted, banging his fist on the table, that "they wouldn't dare" and that they were "happy with everything".

"It's revolting," I went on. "Truly horrifying! I'm frightened! And wasn't it strange, later on, how insistent he was about my going to see him?"

"He's not accustomed to rejection."

"Well, my guess is that it's all a lot simpler. I think it's because of the *Russian Word*. He may make out that he doesn't attach any significance to my work there, but you know as well as I do how afraid he is of the press and how he tries to ingratiate himself with it. Maybe he's decided to lure me into becoming one of his myrrh-bearing women.[6] So that I'll write whatever he wants me to write, at his dictation. After all, he does all of his politicking through women. Just think what a trump card he would have in his hands. I think he's got it all figured out very well indeed. He's cunning."

10

Several days after this dinner I had a telephone call from a lady I knew. She reproached me for not coming to a party she had given the evening before and that I'd promised to attend.

I had completely forgotten about this party.

"Vyrubova was there," said the lady. "She was waiting for you. She very much wants to meet you, and I had promised her you would be there. I'm terribly, terribly upset you couldn't come."

"Aha!" I thought. "Messages from the 'other world'. What can she want of me?"

That she was a messenger from that "other world" I didn't doubt for a moment. Two more days went by.

An old friend dropped in on me. She was very flustered.

"S—— is going to have a big party. She's called round a couple of times in person, but you weren't at home. She came to see me earlier today and made me promise to take you with me."

I was rather surprised by S——'s persistence, as I didn't know her so very well. She wasn't hoping to get me to give some kind of a reading, was she? That was the last thing I wanted. I expressed my misgivings.

"Oh no," my friend assured me. "I promise you that she has no hidden designs. S—— is simply very fond of you and would like to see you. Anyway, it should be a very enjoyable evening. There won't be many guests, just friends, because they can't put on grand balls now, not while we're at war. That would be in poor taste. There will be no one there who shouldn't be there—no one superfluous. They're people who know how to give a good party."

11

We arrived after eleven.

There were a lot of people. Among the tail coats and evening dresses were a number of figures in identical black or light-blue domino masks. They were the only ones in fancy dress; it was clear they had come as a group.

My friend took me by the arm and led me to our hostess: "Well, here she is. See? I've brought her with me."

144

A Gypsy was singing in the large ballroom. Short and slight, she was wearing a high-necked dress of shining silk. Her head was thrown back and her dusky face an emblem of suffering as she sang the words:

> In parting she said:
> "Don't you forget me in foreign lands…"

"Just wait a moment," the hostess whispered to me. "She's almost finished."

And she went on standing beside me, evidently looking around for someone.

"Now we can go."

She took my hand and led me across the ballroom, still looking.

Then we entered a small, dimly lit sitting room. There was no one there. The hostess seated me on a sofa. "I'll be back in a moment. Please don't go anywhere."

She did indeed come back in a moment, together with a figure in a black mask.

"This mysterious figure will keep you entertained," said S—— with a laugh. "Please wait for me here."

The black figure sat down beside me and looked silently at me through narrow eye slits.

"You don't know me," it murmured at last, "but I desperately need to speak to you."

It was not a voice I had heard before, but something about its intonations was familiar. It was the same quivering, hysterical tone in which that lady-in-waiting had spoken of Rasputin.

I peered at the woman sitting beside me. No, this wasn't Madame E——. Madame E—— was petite. This lady was very tall. She spoke with a faint lisp, like all of our high society ladies who as children begin speaking English before Russian.

"I know everything," the unknown woman began edgily. "On Thursday you're going to a certain house."

"No," I replied in surprise. "I'm not going anywhere."

She grew terribly flustered. "Why don't you tell me the truth? Why? I know everything."

"Where is it you think I'm going?" I asked.

"There. His place."

"I don't understand a thing."

"Do you mean to test me? All right, I'll say it. On Thursday you're going to… to… Rasputin's."

"What makes you think that? No one has asked me."

The lady fell silent.

"You may not have received the invitation yet… but you soon will. It's already been decided."

"But why does this matter so much to you?" I asked. "Perhaps you could tell me your name?"

"I haven't put on this idiotic mask only to go and tell you my name. And as far as you're concerned, my name is of no importance. It doesn't matter. What matters is that on Thursday you're going to be there."

"I have no intention of going to Rasputin's," I replied calmly. "Of that I can assure you."

"Ah!"

She suddenly leant forward and, with hands tightly encased in black gloves, seized hold of my arm.

"No, you're joking! You will be going! Why wouldn't you?"

"Because it's of no interest to me."

"And you won't change your mind?"

"No."

Her shoulders began to tremble. I thought she was weeping.

"I thought you were someone sincere," she whispered.

I was at a loss.

"What is it you want from me? Does it upset you that I won't be going? I don't understand a thing."

She seized hold of my arm again.

"I implore you by everything you hold sacred—please refuse the invitation. We have to get him to cancel this evening. He mustn't leave Tsarskoye on Thursday. We mustn't let him—or something terrible will happen."

She muttered something, her shoulders quivering.

"I don't see what any of this has to do with me," I said. "But if it will make you feel any better, then please believe me: I give you my word of honour that I won't go. In three days' time I'm going to Moscow."

Again her shoulders began to tremble, and again I thought she was weeping.

"Thank you, my dear one, thank you…"

She quickly bent over and kissed my hand.

Then she jumped up and left.

"No, that can't have been Vyrubova," I thought, remembering how Vyrubova had wanted to see me at that party I hadn't gone to. "No, it wasn't her. Vyrubova is quite plump, and anyway, she limps. It wasn't her."

I found our hostess.

"Who was that masked lady you just brought to me?"

The hostess seemed rather put out.

"How would I know? She was wearing a mask."

While we were at dinner the masked figures seemed to disappear. Or perhaps they had all just taken off their fancy dress.

I spent a long time studying the faces I didn't know, looking for the lips that had kissed my hand...

Sitting at the far end of the table were three musicians: guitar, accordion and tambourine. The very same three musicians. Rasputin's musicians. Here was a link... a thread.

12

The next day Izmailov came over. He was terribly upset.

"Something awful has happened. Here. Read this." And he handed me a newspaper.

In it I read that Rasputin had begun frequenting a literary circle where, over a bottle of wine, he would tell entertaining stories of all kinds about extremely high-ranking figures.

"And that's not the worst of it," said Izmailov. "Filippov came over today and said he'd had an unexpected summons from the secret police, who wanted to know just which literary figures had been to his house and precisely what Rasputin had talked about. Filippov was threatened with exile from Petersburg. But the most astonishing and horrible thing of all is that, there on the interrogator's desk, he could clearly see the guest list, in Manuilov's own hand."

"You're not saying Manuilov works for the secret police, are you?"[7]

"There's no knowing whether it was him or another of Filippov's guests. In any case, we've got to be very careful. Even if they don't interrogate us, they'll be following us. No doubt

about that. So if Rasputin writes to you or summons you by telephone, you'd better not respond. Although he doesn't know your
address, and he's unlikely to have remembered your last name."

"So much for the holy man's mystical secrets! I feel sorry for
Rozanov. What a dull, prosaic ending…"

13

"Madam, some joker's been telephoning. He's rung twice, wanting to speak to you," said my maid, laughing.

"What do you mean, 'some joker'?"

"Well, when I ask, 'Who's calling?' he says, 'Rasputin'. It's
somebody playing the fool."

"Listen, Ksyusha, if this man carries on playing the fool, be
sure to tell him I've gone away, and for a long time. Understand?"

14

I soon left Petersburg. I never saw Rasputin again.

Later, when I read in the papers that his corpse had been
burnt, the man I saw in my mind's eye was that black, bent,
terrible sorcerer:

"Burn me? Let them. But there's one thing they don't know:
if they kill Rasputin, it will be the end of Russia."

"Remember me then! Remember me!"

I did.

1924
Translated by Anne Marie Jackson

We Are Still Living

Everything is cold and awful. The electricity is only on for five hours a day. There's no firewood. The buildings are barely heated. These great hulks of stone, six-storeys high, are now so icy that they seem to breathe out cold as you walk past.

And there's something new to be seen on the streets: the bourgeoisie are now shovelling snow and selling newspapers.

Nothing, it seems, can unsettle these people.

The ladies have run up special outfits for working outside: peasant-style jackets and sheepskin coats—*tulups* and *zipuns*.[1] Dressmakers call these new costumes *"façon touloup* and *façon zipoun* à la street-sweeper"* and charge through the nose for them.

Those Bolsheviks in the Smolny are a crafty lot.[2] They've decreed that every woman under forty must report for snow-shovelling duty. What woman is fool enough to tell the whole world she's over forty? So far, not a single one has owned up. Instead, they've all been throwing themselves into the fray. It's rumoured that many women have tried to bribe the housing committees into putting them on the roster for snow-shovelling. The committees' response is:

"Go on then, if you're sure it won't finish you off."

The bourgeois selling newspapers are quite happy with their lot. Most of them are ex-army officers.

They sell the evening papers. They stand on Nevsky Prospekt and call out their wares in cheerful, ringing tones. Hearing the cry of a seasoned newspaper-seller, you turn round and, to your surprise, see the kangaroo-fur[3] collar of a former officer and find yourself looking into a pair of intelligent eyes.

The real newspaper-sellers don't like this: "This business isn't for the likes of you."

To which the officer will reply, "And is that any business of yours?"

These bourgeois newspaper-sellers are happy. They earn fifteen roubles a day (more than they could have earned in their wildest dreams) and what's more, they don't have to get up early in the morning.

It's good to be out on the street in the daytime. In the centre of town there is almost no robbing or looting. In shop windows you sometimes come across relics of hoary antiquity: teacups and shirt collars. Or you might catch sight of a little sign: "The latest thing—Stockings!" In bookshops you will find—(ha ha)—books and novels. There was indeed a time when people read novels about young ladies called Vera who sat around all day struggling to understand their true identities. Just look at these Veras now!

Yes, the streets are not bad at all in the daytime. Especially if you just stand still. Walking anywhere is impossible. Even the cabmen's horses have trouble negotiating the great blocks of ice, the mountains of snow and the quiet valleys between them. But if you just stand still, it's really not too bad.

"And where are you off to in such a hurry?"

"Home."

"Why bother? If you go back home, you might get your throat cut."

They say the city will empty out soon—half the population will have left. A new decree states that all looters and criminals must leave the city immediately.

A lot of people are jealous: all the trouble you have to go to in order to get permission to travel and now, all of a sudden, the door is wide open, if you please.

And the government's generosity to the looters is unlikely to stop there. Disbanding this army of bandits will take more than one day. The looters are going to need some help to obey the decree.

First of all, the government should lay on special trains, with the time and route specified: "First Looters' Express"; "Looters' Train B"; "Looters' Medical"; "Looters' Supply Train" (because, after all, looters have to eat too); "Kislovodsk Looters' Train"; "Deluxe Looters' Express". Or simplest of all, suspend all passenger and goods trains, and arrange a "Looters' Week".

Otherwise nothing will come of it.

For the time being, "due to the lack of transport", the robbers go on robbing.

If several robbers attack one passer-by, this is called the "socialization of capital".[4]

But if one person attacks several passers-by, this is ideologically unsound and is called "capitalist individualization".[5]

Apparently a set of rules has been published, stating which streets may be walked along at which time.

Although, it has to be said, there are some streets that should not be walked along at any time.

During the last pogrom,[6] a service was being held in the church on Voskresensky Prospect. As the service was ending, there was the sound of shooting out in the street. A report was sent to the Smolny, following which a guard was dispatched to escort the congregation and the clergy back to their homes.

I don't imagine that the clergy felt entirely comfortable to be availing themselves of the services of the Bolsheviks.

"If you would be so good as to accompany me home, dear brother-anathema."[7]

Each member of the clergy was seen to his door by four anathemas.

For some time now there's been no shooting at all. It's very quiet. This unaccustomed silence makes our ears ring.

It's dark. And it's cold.

"It's a dog's life, my dear chap," I heard a man on the tram complaining. His ears were stuffed with cotton wool. "A dog's life. You run around all day like a dog, sniffing about for a bone. You grab your bone and drag it home. You snarl at anyone who tries to take it. You gnaw at it, wrap the leftovers in some rags and bury them, just like a dog, so no one can take them. And then again, at night, you sit at your gate like a dog, guarding your house—that is, if you still have bread in the house to guard: the third of an ounce that remains from your four-ounce ration of bread made from straw."[8]

Not long ago, a man got a splinter in his tongue from the bread. His tongue swelled up and he died. People had a good laugh. And he chose the wrong time, too. The very next day he could have got an egg on his ration card.

All that was a long time ago, needless to say. About ten days ago. Now it sounds like some fairy story.

The only people who can get eggs now are children. Four children are entitled to one egg between them, once a year.

That's how we live. A lot of people are starting to think that we aren't living, but quite simply dying. But then, when people are very hungry and very cold, and unhappy into the bargain, it's probably all too easy for them to imagine they're dying.

On the other hand...

Dear God, if it's all the same to you, let us die a warm death.

Written in 1918, but published only posthumously
Translated by Rose France

The Gadarene Swine

There are not many of them, of these refugees from Sovietdom. A small group of people with nothing in common; a small motley herd huddled by the cliff's edge before the final leap. Creatures of different breeds and with coats of different colours, entirely alien to one another, with natures that have perhaps always been mutually antagonistic, they have wandered off together and collectively refer to themselves as "we". They have wandered off for no purpose, for no reason. Why?

The legend of the country of the Gadarenes comes to mind. Men possessed by demons came out from among the tombs, and Christ healed them by driving the demons into a herd of swine, and the swine plunged from a cliff and drowned.

Herds of a single animal are rare in the East. More often they are mixed. And in the herd of Gadarene swine there were evidently some meek, frightened sheep. Seeing the crazed swine hurtling along, these sheep took to their heels too.

"Is that *our* lot?"

"Yes, they're running for it!"

And the meek sheep plunged down after the swine and they all perished together.

Had dialogue been possible in the course of this mad dash, it might have resembled what we've been hearing so often in recent days:

"Why are we running?" ask the meek.

"Everyone's running."

"Where are we running to?"

"Wherever everyone else is running."

"What are we doing with *them*? They're not our kind of people. We shouldn't be here with them. Maybe we ought to have stayed where we were. Where the men possessed by demons were coming out from the tombs. What are we doing? We've lost our way, we don't know what we're…"

But the swine running alongside them know very well what they're doing. They egg the meek on, grunting "Culture! We're running towards culture! We've got money sewn into the soles of our shoes. We've got diamonds stuck up our noses. Culture! Culture! Yes, we must save our culture!"

They hurtle on. Still on the run, they speculate. They buy up, they buy back, they sell on. They peddle rumours. The fleshy disc at the end of a pig's snout may only look like a five-kopek coin, but the swine are selling them now for a hundred roubles.

"Culture! We're saving culture! For the sake of culture!"

"How very strange!" say the meek. "'Culture' is our kind of word. It's a word we use ourselves. But now it sounds all wrong. Who is it you're running away from?"

"The Bolsheviks."

"How very strange!" the meek say sadly. "Because we're running away from the Bolsheviks, too."

If the swine are fleeing the Bolsheviks, then it seems that the meek should have stayed behind.

But they're in headlong flight. There's no time to think anything through.

They are indeed all running away from the Bolsheviks. But the crazed swine are escaping from Bolshevik *truth*, from socialist *principles*, from equality and justice, while the meek and frightened are escaping from *untruth*, from Bolshevism's black reality, from terror, injustice and violence.

"What was there for me to do back there?" asks one of the meek. "I'm a professor of international law. I could only have died of hunger."

Indeed, what is there for a professor of international law to do—a man whose professional concern is the inviolability of principles that no longer exist? What use is he now? All he can do is give off an air of international law. And now he's on the run. During the brief stops he hurries about, trying to find someone in need of his international law. Sometimes he even finds a bit of work and manages to give a few lectures. But then the crazed swine break loose and sweep him along behind them.

"We have to run. Everyone is running."

Out-of-work lawyers, journalists, artists, actors and public figures—they're all on the run.

"Maybe we should have stayed behind and fought?"

Fought? But how? Make wonderful speeches when there's no one to hear them? Write powerful articles that there's nowhere to publish?

"And who should we have fought against?"

Should an impassioned knight enter into combat with a windmill, then—and please remember this—the windmill will always win. Even though this certainly does not mean—and please remember this too—that the windmill is right.

They're running. They're in torment, full of doubt, and they're on the run.

Alongside them, grunting and snorting and not doubting anything, are the speculators, former gendarmes, former Black Hundreds[1] and a variety of other former scoundrels. Former though they may be, these groups retain their particularities.

There are heroic natures who stride joyfully and passionately through blood and fire towards—*ta-rum-pum-pum!*—a new life!

And there are tender natures who are willing, with no less joy and no less passion, to sacrifice their lives for what is most wonderful and unique, but without the *ta-rum-pum-pum*. With a prayer rather than a drum roll.

Wild screams and bloodshed extinguish all light and colour from their souls. Their energy fades and their resources vanish. The rivulet of blood glimpsed in the morning at the gates of the commissariat, a rivulet creeping slowly across the pavement, cuts across the road of life for ever. It's impossible to step over it.

It's impossible to go any farther. Impossible to do anything but turn and run.

And so these tender natures run.

The rivulet of blood has cut them off for ever, and they shall never return.

Then there are the more everyday people, those who are neither good nor bad but entirely average, the all too real people who make up the bulk of what we call humanity. The ones for whom science and art, comfort and culture, religion and laws were created. Neither heroes nor scoundrels—in a word, just plain ordinary people.

To exist without the everyday, to hang in the air without any familiar footing—with no sure, firm earthly footing—is something only heroes and madmen can do.

A "normal person" needs the trappings of life, life's earthly flesh—that is, the everyday.

Where there's no religion, no law, no conventions, no settled routine (even if only the routine of a prison or a penal camp), an ordinary, everyday person cannot exist.

At first he'll try to adapt. Deprived of his breakfast roll, he'll eat bread; deprived of bread, he'll settle for husks full of grit; deprived of husks, he'll eat rotten herring—but he'll eat all of this with the same look on his face and the same attitude as if he were eating his usual breakfast roll.

But what if there's nothing to eat at all? He loses his way, his light fades, the colours of life turn pale for him.

Now and then there's a brief flicker from some tremulous beam of light.

"Apparently *they* take bribes too! Did you know? Have you heard?"

The happy news takes wing, travelling by word of mouth—a promise of life, like "Christ is Risen!"

Bribery! The everyday, the routine, a way of life we know as our own! Something earthly and solid!

But bribery alone does not allow you to settle down and thrive.

You must run. In pursuit of your daily bread in the biblical sense of the word: food, clothing, shelter, and labour that provides these things and law that protects them.

Children must acquire the knowledge needed for work, and people of mature years must apply this knowledge to the business of everyday life.

So it has always been, and it cannot of course be otherwise.

There are heady days in the history of nations—days that have to be lived through, but that one can't go on living in for ever.

"Enough carousing—time to get down to work."

Does this mean, then, that we have to do things in some new way? What time should we go to work? What time should we have lunch? Which school should we prepare the children for? We're ordinary people, the levers, belts, screws, wheels and drives of a vast machine; we're the core, the very thick of humanity—what do you want us to do?

"We want you to do all manner of foolish things. Instead of screws we'll have belts, we'll use belts to screw in nuts. And levers instead of wheels. And a wheel will do the job of a belt. Impossible? Outdated prejudice! At the sharp end of a bayonet, nothing is impossible. A theology professor can bake gingerbread and a porter give lectures on aesthetics. A surgeon can sweep the street and a laundress preside over the courtroom."

"We're afraid! We can't do it, we don't know how. A porter lecturing on aesthetics may believe in the value of what he is doing, but a professor baking gingerbread knows only too well that his gingerbread may be anything under the sun—but it certainly isn't gingerbread."

Take to your heels! Run!

Somewhere over there… in Kiev… in Yekaterinburg… in Odessa… some place where children are studying and people are working, it'll still be possible to live a little… For the time being.

And so on they run.

But they are few and they are becoming fewer still. They're growing weak, falling by the wayside. They're running after a way of life that is itself on the run.

And now that the motley herd has wandered onto the Gadarene cliff for its final leap, we can see how very small it is. It could be gathered up into some little ark and sent out to sea. But there the seven unclean pairs would devour the seven clean pairs and then die of overeating.[2]

And the souls of the clean would weep over the dead ark:

"It grieves us to have suffered the same fate as the unclean, to have died together with them on the ark."

Yes, my dears. There's not much you can do about it. You'll all die together. Some from eating, some from being eaten. But "impartial history" will make no distinction. You will all be numbered together.

"And the entire herd plunged from the cliff and drowned."

March 1919
Translated by Anne Marie Jackson

PART IV

Artists and Writers Remembered

My First Tolstoy

I remember... I'm nine years old.

I'm reading *Childhood* by Tolstoy. Over and over again.

Everything in this book is dear to me.

Volodya, Nikolenka and Lyubochka are all living with me; they're all just like me and my brothers and sisters. And their home in Moscow with their grandmother is our Moscow home; when I read about their drawing room, morning room or classroom, I don't have to imagine anything—these are all our own rooms.

I know Natalya Savishna, too. She's our old Avdotya Matveyevna, Grandmother's former serf. She too has a trunk with pictures glued to the top. Only she's not as good-natured as Natalya Savishna. She likes to grumble. "Nor was there anything in nature he ever wished to praise." So my older brother used to sum her up, quoting from Pushkin's "The Demon".

Nevertheless, the resemblance is so pronounced that every time I read about Natalya Savishna, I picture Avdotya Matveyevna.

Every one of these people is near and dear to me.

Even the grandmother—peering with stern, questioning eyes from under the ruching of her cap, a bottle of eau de cologne on the little table beside her chair—even the grandmother is near and dear to me.

The only alien element is the tutor, Saint-Jérôme, whom Nikolenka and I both hate. Oh, how I hate him! I hate him even more and longer than Nikolenka himself, it seems, because Nikolenka eventually buries the hatchet, but I go on hating him for the rest of my life.

Childhood became part of my own childhood and girlhood, merging with it seamlessly, as though I wasn't just reading but truly living it.

But what pierced my heart in its first flowering, what pierced it like a red arrow was another work by Tolstoy—*War and Peace*.

I remember…

I'm thirteen years old.

Every evening, at the expense of my homework, I'm reading one and the same book over and over again—*War and Peace*.

I'm in love with Prince Andrei Bolkonsky. I hate Natasha, first because I'm jealous, second because she betrayed him.

"You know what?" I tell my sister. "I think Tolstoy got it wrong when he was writing about her. How could anyone possibly like her? How could they? Her braid was 'thin and short', her lips were puffy. No, I don't think anyone could have liked her. And if Prince Andrei was going to marry her, it was because he felt sorry for her."

It also bothered me that Prince Andrei always shrieked when he was angry. I thought Tolstoy had got it wrong here, too. I felt certain the Prince didn't shriek.

And so every evening I was reading *War and Peace*.

The pages leading up to the death of Prince Andrei were torture to me.

I think I always nursed a little hope of some miracle. I must have done, because each time he lay dying I felt overcome by the same despair.

Lying in bed at night, I would try to save him. I would make him throw himself to the ground along with everyone else when the grenade was about to explode. Why couldn't just one soldier think to push him out of harm's way? That's what I'd have done. I'd have pushed him out of the way all right.

Then I would have sent him the very best doctors and surgeons of the time.

Every week I would read that he was dying, and I would hope and pray for a miracle. I would hope and pray that maybe this time he wouldn't die.

But he did. He died. And died again.

A living person dies once, but Prince Andrei was dying forever, forever.

My heart ached. I couldn't do my homework. And in the morning... Well, you know what it's like in the morning when you haven't done your homework!

Finally, I hit upon an idea. I decided to go and see Tolstoy and ask him to save Prince Andrei. I would even allow him to marry the Prince to Natasha. Yes, I was even prepared to agree to that—anything to save him from dying!

I asked my governess whether a writer could change something in a work he had already published. She said she thought he probably could—sometimes writers make amendments in later editions.

I conferred with my sister. She said that when you called on a writer you had to bring a small photograph of him and ask him to autograph it, or else he wouldn't even talk to you. Then she said that writers didn't talk to juveniles anyway.

It was very intimidating.

Gradually I worked out where Tolstoy lived. People were telling me different things—one person said he lived in Khamovniki, another said he'd left Moscow, and someone else said he would be leaving any day now.

I bought the photograph and started to think about what to say. I was afraid I might just start crying. I didn't let anyone in the house know about my plans—they would have laughed at me.

Finally, I took the plunge. Some relatives had come for a visit and the household was a flurry of activity—it seemed a good moment. I asked my elderly nanny to walk me "to a friend's house to do some homework" and we set off.

Tolstoy was at home. The few minutes I spent waiting in his foyer were too short to orchestrate a getaway. And with my nanny there it would have been awkward.

I remember a stout lady humming as she walked by. I certainly wasn't expecting that. She walked by entirely naturally. She wasn't afraid, and she was even humming. I had thought everyone in Tolstoy's house would walk on tiptoe and speak in whispers.

Finally *he* appeared. He was shorter than I'd expected. He looked at Nanny, then at me. I held out the photograph and, too scared to be able to pronounce my "R"s, I mumbled, "Would you pwease sign your photogwaph?"

He took it out of my hand and went into the next room.

At this point I understood that I couldn't possibly ask him for anything and that I'd never dare say why I'd come. With my "pwease" and "photogwaph" I had brought shame on myself. Never, in his eyes, would I be able to redeem myself. Only by the grace of God would I get out of here in one piece.

He came back and gave me the photograph. I curtsied.

"What can I do for you, madam?" he asked Nanny.

"Nothing, sir, I'm here with the young lady, that's all."

Later on, lying in bed, I remembered my "pwease" and "photogwaph" and cried into my pillow.

At school I had a rival named Yulenka Arsheva. She, too, was in love with Prince Andrei, but so passionately that the whole class knew about it. She, too, was angry with Natasha Rostova and she, too, could not believe that the Prince shrieked.

I was taking great care to hide my own feelings. Whenever Yulenka grew agitated, I tried to keep my distance and not listen to her so that I wouldn't betray myself.

And then, one day, during literature class, our teacher was analysing various literary characters. When he came to Prince Bolkonsky, the class turned as one to Yulenka. There she sat, red-faced, a strained smile on her lips and her ears so suffused with blood that they even looked swollen.

Their names were now linked. Their romance evoked mockery, curiosity, censure, intense personal involvement—the whole gamut of attitudes with which society always responds to any romance.

I alone did not smile—I alone, with my secret, "illicit" feeling, did not acknowledge Yulenka or even dare look at her.

In the evening I sat down to read about his death. But now I read without hope. I was no longer praying for a miracle.

I read with feelings of grief and suffering, but without protest. I lowered my head in submission, kissed the book and closed it.

There once was a life. It was lived out, and it ended.

1920

Translated by Anne Marie Jackson

The Merezhkovskys

A dead man can't be flattered.

—RADISHCHEV

People who knew Dmitry Merezhkovsky and Zinaida Gippius well do not write very warmly of them in their memoirs.

Andrei Bely writes that Merezhkovsky wore shoes with pompoms, and that these pompoms epitomized the whole of Merezhkovsky's life. Both his speech and his thought had "pompoms".[1]

Not the most precise of descriptions, but certainly not a very kind one. Though Andrei Bely was not without "pompoms" of his own.

Alexei Remizov calls Merezhkovsky a walking coffin, and says that "Zinaida Nikolaevna Gippius was all bones and springs—a complex mechanical apparatus—but it was impossible to think of her as a living human being. With stinging malice they rejected every manifestation of life."

The complex mechanical apparatus called Zinaida Gippius was in fact a great deal more complex than "bones and springs".

I've more than once had occasion to read extremely spiteful literary reminiscences about "friends". Something along the lines of an earthly Last Judgment. A man is stripped of all his coverings and ornaments and his naked corpse is dragged out into the open to be ridiculed.

This is cruel and wrong. We must not forget how difficult it is to be a human being.

After reading memoirs like this, one writer recently said, "You know, for the first time in my life, I've felt terrified by the thought of dying."

And I was reminded of a sweet lady from Petersburg who said of a friend, "There's nothing this woman won't stoop to if she thinks she'll gain by it. You can take my word for it—I'm her best friend."

Trying to describe Dmitry Sergeyevich Merezhkovsky and Zinaida Nikolaevna Gippius really is very difficult.

Each was one of a kind, completely out of the ordinary— the usual yardsticks did not apply to them. Their literary gifts aside—considered simply as people—each could have been the central character in a long psychological novel.

Their extraordinary, almost tragic egocentricity was understandable once one had found the key to it. This key was their utter detachment from everyone else, a detachment that seemed innate and which they had no compunctions about. Like Gogol's Khoma Brut, who had drawn a circle around himself.[2] Neither howling demons nor the flying coffin of a dead sorceress could touch him. He felt cold and he was alone, although there was nothing but a circle separating him—and separating the Merezhkovskys—from people and life. When the Merezhkovskys felt frightened, they briskly sought the help of holy intercessors. They decorated their statuette of

Saint Theresa with flowers and, with neither faith nor divine inspiration, mumbled their way through their invocations. On Dmitry Sergeyevich's death, Zinaida Nikolaevna felt so upset with Saint Theresa for allowing this bad thing to happen that she threw a shawl over the statuette and stood it in the corner. Just like a savage who smears his deity with fat when things go well, and flogs it in the event of misfortune. That is just the way she was. And—at the same time—Zinaida Gippius was an intelligent, subtle and talented poet. An extraordinary combination. She was indeed one of a kind.

When he was told that war had been declared, Dmitry Sergeyevich observed perfectly coolly, "Ah well—but I think the trains will keep running."

The trains would keep running—and he would be able to take himself off somewhere far, far away, so that the circle he had drawn would not be broken, so that he, Merezhkovsky, would not feel the touch of hard, wicked life; and as for what lay out there, beyond the magic circle—cold, hunger, violence and death—that would be other people's concern, it wouldn't touch him.

The Merezhkovskys led strange lives and were so out of touch with reality that it was positively startling to hear them come out with ordinary words like "coal", "boiled water" and "macaroni". The word "ink" was less startling—at least it had to do with writing and ideas... They both lived in the world of ideas, and they were unable to see or in any way understand either people or life itself. You won't find a single real person in any of their writings. Zinaida Gippius freely acknowledged this, saying that the actors in her stories were not people but ideas.

Since I don't intend to discuss their literary work but simply to describe the Merezhkovskys as they appeared to me, this peculiarity of theirs might seem irrelevant—but it did in fact play a crucial role in their whole approach to people and life.

All around them were scarcely perceptible shades, phantoms and spectres. These shades had names and they spoke, though what they said had no meaning. As for Merezhkovsky, he never conversed. Dialogue meant nothing to him. The Merezhkovskys never knew what any particular person felt about them, nor did they have the least wish to know. They could be attentive (Merezhkovsky could even be absurdly flattering) to someone useful, but without taking any real interest in this person or why they might want to make themselves useful to him.

As to whether they had ever felt simple human love towards someone… I doubt it.

At one time they were very good friends with Dmitry Filosofov. For a long time they formed an inseparable trio.

When a rumour went round Biarritz that Filosofov had died, I thought, "Someone is going to have to tell the Merezhkovskys."

That day I happened to meet them on the street.

"Have you heard the sad news about Filosofov?"

"What news? Has he died?" asked Merezhkovsky.

"Yes."

"Do they know what from?" he asked. And without waiting for an answer, he said, "Well, we must be on our way, Zina, or we'll be late again and all the best dishes will be gone."

"We're having lunch at a restaurant today," he explained.

And that was that.

In Petersburg I had only seldom come across the Merezhkovskys. We didn't get to know one another at all well until our time in Biarritz.[3] There we saw a lot of one another and talked a great deal.

Life did not go well for the Merezhkovskys in Biarritz. It was not easy for any of us, but it must have been especially hard for them, since they took any kind of disorder in their living arrangements as a personal affront.

We refugees had been allocated the magnificent Maison Basque hotel. Each of us had a beautifully appointed room and bathroom for ten francs a day. But the Merezhkovskys were reluctant to pay even this. They considered it unjust. All their practical affairs were seen to by their secretary, Vladimir Zlobin, a touchingly steadfast friend. A talented poet himself, Zlobin had abandoned literature in order to fully devote himself to looking after the Merezhkovskys.

Money, of course, was tight, and we had to be inventive. A grand fundraising celebration was arranged for Dmitry Sergeyevich's seventy-fifth birthday.[4]

Presided over by Countess G., the guests—some wearing German uniforms—assembled on the enormous terrace of our hotel. Merezhkovsky gave a long speech that greatly alarmed all the Russians living in the hotel. In this speech he attacked both the Bolsheviks and the Germans. He trusted that the present nightmare would soon be over, that the antichrists terrorizing Russia and the antichrists that now had France by the throat would soon be destroyed, and that the Russia of Dostoevsky would hold out a hand to the France of Pascal and Joan of Arc.

"Now the Germans will throw us out of the hotel," the Russians whispered fearfully.

But the Germans seemed not to understand Merezhkovsky's prophecies and they applauded genially along with everyone else. They did not throw us out of the hotel. Nevertheless, we were unable to stay there long. The hotel was to be made into an army barracks and we all had to find rooms in private apartments.

The Merezhkovskys managed to install themselves in a wonderful villa, which naturally they could not afford. Dmitry Sergeyevich was ill; it was thought he had a stomach ulcer. And Zinaida Nikolaevna was nursing him dutifully.

"I changed his hot water bottle seventeen times last night," she said. "Then old age got the better of me and I emptied out the eighteenth onto my stomach."

Despite his illness, they continued to receive people on Sundays. Chatting and joking, everyone would sit in the large dining room, around an empty table. Merezhkovsky was usually at the far end of the room, reclining on a chaise longue, sullen and sulking. He would greet his guests by shouting loudly, "There's no tea. No tea at all."

"Look, Madam D. has brought us some biscuits," said Zinaida Nikolaevna.

"Let them bring biscuits. Let them bring everything!" Merezhkovsky declared grimly.

"But Dmitry Sergeyevich," I said. "I thought suffering ennobled the soul." I had heard these words from him many times.

"Indeed it does!" he barked—and turned away. I think he found me almost unbearable. When he spoke to me he never looked at me, and when, in my presence, he spoke about me, he would refer to me simply as *she*. It was quite amusing, really.

After I had packed everything in preparation for the move, I went down to the Merezhkovskys and asked Zinaida Nikolaevna if she could lend me a book for the night. They always had piles of cheap French crime novels which they read diligently every evening.

"Zina," said Merezhkovsky, "grab one from the second-rate pile and say she absolutely must return it tomorrow morning."

"No," I said to Zinaida Nikolaevna. "*She* is going to choose something she likes and bring it back in her own good time. *She* is certainly not going to hurry."

He turned away angrily.

Zinaida Nikolaevna courteously found me one of the more interesting books.

Another time, while we were still at the hotel, I found a letter under my door. The Merezhkovskys and I were being invited to move to the Free Zone. Well-wishers had arranged visas for us and would pay our passage to America. I was to inform the Merezhkovskys at once. And so, off I went.

Merezhkovsky was furious.

"She must tell them to keep their distance. And she's not to go either."

"Why should *she* be so rude to people who are only showing their concern and doing their best to help?" I asked.

"They're not trying to help us at all, and they're not in the least concerned about us. They only want our names. I'd rather go to Spain. They've got a saint there that hardly anyone has written anything about. I'll write a book about her and they'll give me a visa. But *she* should stay here in Biarritz."

"More saints?" I asked. "You're a real demon, Dmitry Sergeyevich—you can't keep away from saints."

Strangely, though, despite his loathing for *her* (a loathing well earned, as I could never resist teasing him), they had somehow taken it into their heads that they'd like to move into an apartment with me. This plan greatly amused the rest of the Russian colony. Everyone was wondering exactly how this arrangement would work out.

During these first months the Merezhkovskys felt a real disgust for the Germans, which they made no attempt to hide. If we were about to go out together, Zinaida Nikolaevna would begin with a quick check: were there any Germans about? If she did see a German, she would slam the gate and wait for him to pass by. And she drew caricatures of the Germans that were really not bad at all.

The Merezhkovskys led a very ordered existence. Dmitry Sergeyevich worked throughout the morning and rested after an early lunch. Then they would always go for a walk.

"A walk is the light of day; a day with no walk—pitch darkness," he liked to say.

His spine was completely bent. My impression was that he found even standing difficult unless he had something to lean on or a wall to rest against. And so Zinaida Nikolaevna always had to lead him determinedly along, supporting nearly all his weight on her arm. This was something she was so accustomed to that when she and I went out together, she always asked me to take her arm and give her more of my weight.

Very gradually the Merezhkovskys began to allow the Germans into their lives. There were young Germans, students, who wanted to pay their respects to a writer whose work they had read in translation. They would ask in reverent tones for his autograph. Merezhkovsky would never engage in conversation with them. Occasionally, however, he would shout in Russian: "Tell them to bring some cigarettes with them!" or "Tell them we need eggs!" Zinaida Nikolaevna would talk to them now and again, though she never said anything very nice to them.

"You're all like machines. The bosses command—and you obey."

"But of course we do, we're soldiers. We have our discipline. What do you expect us to do?"

"Nevertheless, you're machines."

I would needle her.

"I suppose you'd like them to form a Soviet of Soldiers' Deputies? Under a banner with the slogan 'To Hell with all Officers!'"

"Nevertheless, they're machines."

She was not easily diverted.

The Germans' conduct in Biarritz was not exactly exemplary. Towards those who fawned over them, they were extremely polite and obliging. The rest of us they simply ignored, as if we were transparent. They would look through us and see a house, a crowd, a landscape. It feels strange to be so very transparent.

There was one especially important German. He wore a military uniform, but it seemed that before the war he had been a banker. I can no longer remember his exact political or military position, but, judging by the number of people eager to ingratiate themselves with him, it must have been something important. He had only to walk into a café and Biarritz's lady aristocrats—the *Duchesse de*, the *Contesse de* and even some ladies with more than one *de*—would spring to their feet and rush towards him. Their faces were ecstatic and adoring; there were tears in their eyes. I should mention that this German official, a man of mature years, was remarkably ugly. Created along the lines of Gogol's Sobakyevich[5]—whom nature had not given much thought to but had simply hewed out with an axe and decided to leave it at that—this gallant appeared to have been carved, or rather hacked, from tough, resistant wood, and carelessly into the bargain: one nostril was higher, the other lower, one eye was round, the other long. Nor did his appearance seem to matter very much to him. But it was obvious that the inordinate admiration of the Biarritz ladies was starting to go to his head. The old Countess G., the organizer of Merezhkovsky's birthday celebration, said that she had been truly stunned by this German's remarkable looks. "Like the knight in the engraving by Dürer!" she had kept exclaiming.

The ladies corrupted the poor German to such a degree that he began acting precious and coy. He was once seen playing with a little dog on the town square, offering it a lump of sugar. He would smile and bend down, then pull his hand away to tease the dog. He was like a spoilt, capricious ballet-dancer whose impresario is infatuated with him.

At some point during the winter his wife appeared. She had heard that a French countess, a lady who moved in the highest society, was rather taken with her husband.

"Is it true she's no longer young?" she asked.

"Oh yes," replied the German. "She must be over sixty."

"Very true," said a Frenchman who was also party to this conversation. "She certainly is over sixty. She's eighty-seven."

This positively frightened the German. He blinked several times and asked for this number to be translated for him. The number was duly translated. After many shakes of the head, he said, "This could only happen in France."

The countess certainly knew how to bewilder. She would flash her dark eyes, wag a warning finger, or impatiently tap her little foot. This little foot, with its flat sole and its gnarled and hooked elderly toes, resembled nothing so much as a rake, but the countess decked it out in the most youthful manner. She felt she was young and enchanting. If she heard someone speak admiringly of a young woman from her circle, she would feel deeply upset. Her lady companion all but wept: "All night long she kept waking me up and shouting, 'How could he find *her* beautiful in *my* presence. In *my* presence?'"

I asked Zinaida Nikolaevna, "What do you think? Is she a witch?"

"Of course she's a witch."

"Do you think she flies out through the chimney at night?"

"Of course she does."

"On a broomstick?"

"How else?"

Among the other astonishing characters flitting around Biarritz there was a very amusing Belgian woman who had something to do with the Red Cross. That at least is what she told us—and perched on her mighty bosom, on the stained grey wool into which it had been squeezed, was some kind of badge. This lady drank immoderately and wrote love letters to the elderly countess, imploring her for material assistance. The letters began with the words: "*Votre Beauté!*"

The countess did not deny the woman the help she asked for, but to her friends she said, "I must admit I am quite afraid to be left alone with her. She gives me such passionate looks."

This remarkable countess had also taken Dmitry Sergeyevich under her wing—though she took no interest in Zinaida Nikolaevna, whom she merely tolerated as a writer's wife. As a rule, she disliked women. Women were rivals: well-bred gentlemen are unfailingly courteous to women, and the countess wished to reign supreme. She introduced the Merezhkovskys to the German who resembled the engraving by Dürer, organized breakfast parties and made plans for all kinds of unusual lectures, talks and outings. It was around this time that the Nazi–Soviet pact broke down. Merezhkovsky then boldly affirmed what was to become his motto: "If the Devil is against the Bolsheviks, you should ally yourself with the Devil." The Germans, of course, were the Devil.

The countess's plans were indeed brilliant, but money was still very tight.

I remember once going to a café. Seated at a small table by the window were the Merezhkovskys. Not noticing me, they carried on with their conversation. Zinaida Nikolaevna had very poor hearing and Merezhkovsky's voice filled the room: "They've cut off our electricity. Vladimir has been all over the town looking for candles, but there are none anywhere. We're going to end up sitting in the dark."

He was very agitated. His teaspoon was trembling in his hand and rattling against his cup. There were red blotches on his pale cheeks. And I knew that there were indeed no candles to be found anywhere in Biarritz.

They were always irritated, astonished, even sincerely out-raged by the need to pay bills. Zinaida Nikolaevna told me indignantly about how they had just had a visit from the man who hired out bed linen.

"The scoundrel just won't leave us alone. Yesterday he was told that we were out, so he sat in the garden and waited for us. Thanks to that scoundrel we couldn't even go for a walk."

There was such childlike naivety in Zinaida Nikolaevna's irritation that one's sympathy always went to her rather than to the man whose bill had not been paid.

Thanks to the countess's influence, Merezhkovsky was given permission to give a lecture in a public hall. The audience was small, and included several German officers who were clearly there in an official capacity. Merezhkovsky spoke so softly that I could barely hear him, even though I was in the front row. I told him as much during the break.

He took offence. "It doesn't matter. I refuse to speak more loudly. It'll spoil my modulations. My modulations are superb. I've taken great pains over them."

In the second half he simply whispered. The Germans got up and left. Recently the countess had grown somewhat less interested in Merezhkovsky. She had more important business to attend to. She was elaborating a plan to save France. It was not the first time she had done this. There had been an earlier occasion when, as she liked to tell us, she had balanced the state budget. How? By arranging greyhound races that had brought the government billions of francs in revenue.

Under the countess's influence, Merezhkovsky had become more gracious towards the Germans (the devils opposing the Bolsheviks). He had even come to see Hitler as a kind of Napoleon.

"Zinaida Nikolaevna! What is it? What's got into him?" I asked.

"He's a sycophant. He's the son of a minor palace official. That's why he grovels. First before Piłsudski, then before Mussolini. Pure sycophantism."

Harsh, but all too true, I fear.

*

Merezhkovsky's appearance was most peculiar. Small and thin, and in his last years bent completely out of shape. What was remarkable, however, was his face. It was deathly pale, with bright red lips—and when he spoke you saw that his gums were the same bright red. There was something frightening about this. Vampire-like.

He never laughed. Neither of them had the least sense of humour. There was something perverse about Merezhkovsky's refusal to understand a joke. Sometimes you would deliberately tell them a very funny story just to see their reaction. Utter bewilderment.

"But his answer's quite wrong," they would say.

"Yes, and that's the point of the story. If his answer had been right, I wouldn't be telling you all this."

"All right, but why did he answer like that?"

"Because he didn't understand."

"Then he's simply a fool. What's so interesting about that?"

Nevertheless Zinaida Nikolaevna did appreciate a few lines from a poem by the genuinely witty and talented Don-Aminado.

> Look before you leap –
> Shoot before you speak.

she would declaim.

Merezhkovsky did not approve.

Zlobin defended Merezhkovsky: "No, he does have a sense of humour. Once he even came up with a play on words."

More than twenty years of close acquaintance—and a

single play on words. Evidently a joker who hid his wit under a bushel.

Zinaida Nikolaevna looked on me with curiosity. To her I was a member of some strange species. She would say, "I absolutely must write about you one day. No one has described you properly yet."

"It's too late," I replied. "I won't be able to act on your suggestions now, and there's no changing the opinions of readers. They all made up their minds about me long ago."

But then a copy of my *Witch*[6] somehow found its way into their hands—and for some reason they both liked it.

"In this volume you're conspiring with eternity," said Zinaida Nikolaevna.

"What language!" said Merezhkovsky. "I'm lapping it up, lapping it up!"

Then he added, "You're nothing like your work. Zina *is* like her work, but you aren't. This book is a delight."

"Heavens!" I exclaimed. "You're trying to tell me that I'm an abomination. How awful. But I don't think there's much we can do about it now."

"But why do you give so much space in your work to the comical? I don't much care for the comical," Merezhkovsky once said to me.

Not "humour", but "the comical". Probably his way of showing contempt.

I reminded him of Gogol's words about humour.

"Listen: 'Laughter is deeper and more significant than people think. At its bottom lies an eternally pulsating spring which lends greater depth to any subject. Even he who fears nothing else on earth fears mockery. Yet there are some who are unaware of laughter's remarkable power. Many say that humour is base; only when something is pronounced in stern, laboured tones do they acknowledge it as sublime.'"[7]

Merezhkovsky was terribly offended: "My tones aren't in the least laboured."

"Of course they aren't. Everyone knows about your modulations. This wasn't written about you."

Zinaida Nikolaevna often quoted from her own poems. Merezhkovsky did not like her recent work.

"Zina, these are not poems."

"Yes, they are," she insisted.

"No, they're not," he shouted.

I intervened: "I think I can reconcile you. Of course they're poems. They have metre and rhyme—all the formal elements of verse. But they're verse rather than poetry, prose thoughts in verse form."

They both accepted this. Now that they had read *Witch*, I was no longer *she* but Teffi.

I remember falling ill and spending nearly a month in bed. The Merezhkovskys visited regularly, and once, to the astonishment of everyone in the room, Dmitry Sergeyevich brought a paper cornet of cherries. He had bought them along the way. We all exchanged glances, our faces all saying the same thing: "And there we were, thinking he has no heart."

Merezhkovsky asked sternly for a dish and said the cherries should be washed.

"Dmitry Sergeyevich," I said sweetly. "It's all right, I'm not frightened. There's no cholera now."

"I know," he said grimly. "But *I'm* still frightened."

He sat in the corner and, noisily spitting out the stones, ate every last cherry. It was so funny that those present were afraid to look at one another lest they burst out laughing.

I was preoccupied by this strange man for a long time. I kept looking for something in him and not finding it. I remembered "Sakya Muni", Merezhkovsky's poem about how the Buddha, the Sage of the Shakhya clan,[8] moved by the suffering of a lowly thief who had said to him "Lord of the World, you are wrong", had bowed his crowned head to the ground. This hymn to humility—from the pen of Merezhkovsky!

And then, one day not long before his death, after they had returned to Paris disappointed by their German patrons and with no money at all—they had even had to sell a gold pen some Italian writers had presented to them during Merezhkovsky's Mussolini period[9]—the three of us were sitting together and Zinaida Nikolaevna remarked of someone, "Yes, people really *do* love him."

"Nonsense!" interrupted Merezhkovsky. "Absolute nonsense! No one loves. No one is loved."

There was something desperate behind this. These were not idle words. Merezhkovsky's whole face had darkened. Dear God! What torments this man must have been going through in the black pit he inhabited… I felt fear for him, and pain.

"Dmitry Sergeyevich! What makes you say that? It's just that you don't see people. You don't really notice them."

"Nonsense. I *do* notice people."

I may be wrong, but in his words I had heard both longing and despair. I thought of his most recent poem, "O Loneliness,

O Poverty". And I thought of Gogol's Khoma Brut. The dead sorceress's coffin flying just above his head. It was terrifying.

"Dmitry Sergeyevich! You truly don't notice people. I know I'm always laughing at you, but really I love you."

It was as if, with these words, I were making the sign of the cross over myself.

For a moment he seemed at a loss; then he recovered himself: "I think it's my works you love—not me."

"No, Dmitry Sergeyevich, I love you, as a human being."

He was silent for a moment. Then he turned and went slowly to his room. He came back and handed me a photograph of himself, with an affectionate inscription.

I have this photograph still.

1950
Translated by Anne Marie Jackson

Ilya Repin

I did not see Repin often. He lived in Finland and came only
seldom to Petersburg.

But one day Kaplan, from the publishing house "Dog Rose", [1]
came round with a letter from Repin. Repin very much liked
my story "The Top". [2] "It moved me to tears," he wrote. And
this had made him want to paint my portrait.

This, of course, was a great honour for me. We agreed on a
date and time, and Kaplan took me along in his car.

It was winter. Cold. Snowstorms. All very miserable. With its
squat dachas deep in snow, Kuokkala was not welcoming. The
sky was also very low, even darker than the earth and breathing
out cold. After Petersburg, with its loud voices, with its whistles
and car horns, the village seemed very quiet. The snow lay in
deep drifts and there could have been a bear beneath every one
of them, fast asleep, sucking its paw.

Repin greeted us warmly. He took us into his studio and
showed us his latest work. Then we sat down for a late breakfast at his famous round table. The table had two levels. On the
top level, which revolved, were all kinds of dishes; you moved
it round and helped yourself to whatever you fancied. On the
lower level were containers for the dirty plates and bowls. It was

all very convenient, and fun—like having a picnic. The food was vegetarian, and there was a lot of variety. Some of our more serious eaters, though, would complain after a visit that they'd been given nothing but hay. In the railway station on the way back home, they'd go to the buffet and fill up on meat rissoles, which would by then have grown cold.

After breakfast—work.

Repin seated me on a little dais and then sat down below me. He was looking up at me, which seemed very strange. I've sat for a number of artists—Alexandr Yakovlev, Savely Sorin, Boris Grigoryev, Savely Schleifer[3] and many who are less well known—but no one has ever gone about it so strangely.

He was using coloured pencils, which he didn't do often. "It'll be Paris style," he said with a smile.

He asked someone else who was there to read aloud "The Top", the story of mine that had made such an impression on him. This made me think of Boris Kustodiev's account of how, while he was painting his portrait of Nicholas II, the Tsar had read aloud one of my stories of village life. He had read well—and then he had asked if it was really true that the author was a lady.

Repin's finished portrait of me was something magically tender, unexpected, not at all like his usual, more forceful work.

He promised to give it to me. But I never received it. It was sent to an exhibition in America and, in Repin's words, "it got stuck in customs".

I didn't like to question him too insistently. "He simply doesn't want to admit that he sold it," people kept telling me.

It would, in any case, have disappeared during the Revolution, as did all the other portraits of me, as did many beloved things without which I'd thought life would be hardly worth living.

Years later, in Paris, I republished "The Top" in *The Book of June*, dedicating the story to Repin. I sent a copy of the book to the address I still had for him in Finland. He replied warmly, asking me to send him a few amateur photographs, just as they were, without any retouching. With these to prompt him, he'd be able to recreate the portrait from memory. At the bottom of the letter was a postscript from his daughter, saying that her father was very weak, hardly able to move about at all.

I was touched by this thoughtfulness on Repin's part, but I was slow to do as he asked. Eventually, however, I did—only to read in a newspaper, the very next day, that Repin had died.

I shall remember this short, rather thin man as someone uncommonly polite and courteous. His manner was always unruffled and he never showed the least sign of irritation. In short: "A man from another age".

I've heard it said that, after pointing out the failings in a work by one of his weaker students, he would add, "Oh, if only I had your brush!"

Even if he didn't really say this, it's easy to imagine him coming out with something similar. Repin was modest. People accustomed to praise and flattery usually speak a lot and don't listen. Speak—rather than converse. Fyodor Chaliapin, Vlas Doroshevich and Leonid Andreyev all strode about the room and held forth. Repin would listen intently to the other person. He conversed.

His wife Natalya Nordman-Severova was a committed vegetarian. She converted her husband. The revolving table was her idea too. When, overcome by jealousy, she left her husband, he remained loyal to vegetarianism. But shortly before his death, growing weaker and weaker, he ate a little curd cheese. This lifted his spirits. Then he decided to eat an egg. And that gave him the strength to get to his feet and even to do some work.[4]

His last note to me read, "I'm waiting for your photos. I'm determined to do your portrait."

His handwriting was weak. He was not strong enough to paint a portrait.

Not that I had ever really expected anything to come of all this. I've never been a collector, never been able to keep hold of things and not let them slip through my hands. When I've been asked by fortune tellers to spread out my palms, they always say, with a shake of the head, "No, with hands like that you'll never be able to hold on to anything."

There was also a portrait of me by Savely Schleifer. It too had its story.[5]

Schleifer had portrayed me in a white tunic and he'd thrown a deep-blue veil over my head.

I had a friend who particularly loved this portrait. He persuaded me to give it to him and he took it to his estate in the province of Kovno.[6] A true aesthete, close to Mikhail Kuzmin, he hung it in the place of honour and always stood a vase of flowers beneath it.

In 1917 he heard that the peasants had looted his house and gone off with all his books and paintings. He hurried back to his estate to try to rescue his treasures.

He managed to track down a few of them. In one hut he found my portrait, hanging in the icon corner beside Saint Nicholas the Miracle Worker and the Iverskaya Mother of

God. Thanks to the long white tunic, the blue veil and the vase of dried flowers, the woman who had taken this portrait had decided I was a saint and lit an icon lamp before me.

A likely story…

The palmists were right. I've never been able to hold on to anything. Neither portraits, nor poems dedicated to me, nor paintings I've been given, nor important letters from interesting people. Nothing at all.

There is a little more preserved in my memory, but even this is gradually, or even rather quickly, losing its meaning, fading, slipping away from me, wilting and dying.

It's sad to wander about the graveyard of my tired memory, where all hurts have been forgiven, where every sin has been more than atoned for, every riddle unriddled and twilight quietly cloaks the crosses, now no longer upright, of graves I once wept over.[7]

Probably written 1950–52
Translated by Robert and Elizabeth Chandler

List of Historical Figures

LEONID ANDREYEV (1871–1919): an acclaimed writer of short stories, plays and novels, one of the most important figures of Russian literature's "Silver Age".

KONSTANTIN BALMONT (1867–1942): one of the founders of Russian Symbolism. He and Teffi's older sister Mirra Lokhvitskaya were intensely—though probably platonically—emotionally involved during the last ten years of her life.

DEMYAN BEDNY (1883–1945): a revolutionary poet and satirist. *Bedny* (a pseudonym) means "poor".

ANDREI BELY (1880–1934): a Symbolist poet and novelist, best known for his novel *Petersburg*.

NIKOLAI BERDYAEV (1874–1948): a religious philosopher. A Marxist as a young man, he went on to adopt a position that has been described as Christian Existentialist. He was expelled from Soviet Russia in 1922.

J.-WLADIMIR BIENSTOCK, né Vladimir Lvovitch Binshtock (1868–1933): a Russian-born writer and translator into French.

ALEXANDER BOGDANOV (1873–1928): a revolutionary and cultural activist, the founder of the proletarian art movement *Proletkult* (1918–20).

VALERY BRYUSOV (1873–1924): a prominent poet and critic, among the founders of Russian Symbolism. One of the few Symbolists to give his wholehearted support to the Soviet regime.

SERGEI BULGAKOV (1871–1944): a theologian. Ordained into the priesthood soon after the Revolution, he was expelled from Russia along with other philosophers and religious thinkers in 1922.

FYODOR CHALIAPIN (1873–1938): one of the most famous operatic basses of his day.

DON-AMINADO, real name Aminodav Shpolyansky (1888–1957): a poet and satirist. Like Teffi, he wrote for *New Satirikon* and other pre-revolutionary journals. Like her, he emigrated to Paris, where he continued to publish poems, articles and stories.

VLAS DOROSHEVICH (1864–1922): a journalist, editor and writer of short stories. Teffi devotes several pages of *Memories* to him.

ANATOLY FARESOV (1852–1928): a member of an older generation of revolutionaries, the "Populist" movement of the 1860s and 1870s.

DMITRY FILOSOFOV (1872–1940): a literary critic, religious thinker and political activist, co-founder and first literary editor of the illustrated journal *Mir iskusstva* (*World of Art*). Close to both Merezhkovsky and Gippius.

ALEXANDER FINN-YENOTAEVSKY (1872–1943): a revolutionary who assumed the pseudonym Yenotaevsky after being exiled for two years to Yenotaevsk in the Arkhangelsk district.

ZINAIDA NIKOLAEVNA GIPPIUS (1869–1945): a Symbolist poet. Along with her husband Dmitry Merezhkovsky, she hosted an important salon. Always flamboyant, she liked to shock both through her behaviour—insulting her guests and wearing male clothes—and through poems that she herself called "personal prayers" but which others saw as blasphemous. She wrote both under her own name and under several male pseudonyms; the best known was "Anton the Extreme". After the Revolution, she and Merezhkovsky settled in Paris. "The Green Lamp", a literary and philosophical society they founded, was attended by many of the most important émigré writers. Teffi ends a separate memoir of Gippius by telling how, after her death, she whispered over her coffin the words, "Friend whom I did not know for long, you did not want to be kind and warm. You wanted to be vicious. Because that is more vivid, isn't it? As for the sweet tenderness that your soul loved in secret, you hid it in embarrassment from the eyes of others."

MAXIM GORKY (1868–1936): claimed by the Soviet regime as the father of Socialist Realism, Gorky published his first book, to great acclaim, in 1898. His subject matter was drawn from the lives of the very lowest social strata. From 1905 until 1918 he was closely involved with Lenin and the Bolsheviks, living for much of this period in Capri. His fame as a writer was worldwide and he was able to provide the Bolsheviks with substantial financial support. In 1918, however, he attacked Lenin and the Soviet regime as criminal and tyrannical; for most of the period from 1921 until 1928 he once again lived in exile. In 1932 he accepted a personal invitation from Stalin to return to the Soviet Union. There he became a (possibly reluctant) cultural figurehead for the Soviet regime.

SERGEI GUSEV (1874–1933): a member of the Bolshevik faction from its inception in 1903.

ALEXANDER IZMAILOV (1873–1921): a journalist and literary critic.

LEV KAMENEV (1883–1936): one of the most important of Lenin's colleagues. A member of the Central Committee during the 1920s, he was shot in 1936, after being sentenced in the first of the Moscow Show Trials.

YEVTIKHY KARPOV (1857–1926): a playwright and theatre director.

MIKHAIL KATKOV (1818–87): a notoriously reactionary journalist.

ALEXANDER KERENSKY (1881–1970): a leading member of the Socialist Revolutionary Party (the SRs); prime minister of the Provisional Government from 8th July until 25th October 1917.

ALEXANDRA KOLLONTAI (1872–1952): a Bolshevik from 1914, famous for her radical views on marriage and sexuality.

ALEXANDER KUGEL (1864–1928): a theatre critic who in 1908 co-founded The Crooked Mirror, a theatre that specialized in parodies and put on two of Teffi's plays.

ALEXANDER KUPRIN (1870–1938): a popular writer of short stories and novels.

BORIS KUSTODIEV (1878–1927): a painter and stage designer. His portrait of Nicholas II, painted in 1915, can be seen in the Russian Museum in St Petersburg.

MIKHAIL KUZMIN (1872–1936): one of the finest poets of his time. He also wrote plays and composed music. In 1906 he published *Wings*, the first Russian novel with an overtly homosexual theme; two large editions sold out at once.

NIKOLAI LEIKIN (1841–1906): editor of *Oskolki* (*Splinters*), the comic journal in which Chekhov published his first stories.

L.A. LINYOV (1853–1920): worked on the *Stock Exchange Gazette* between 1893 and 1896.

MAXIM LITVINOV (1876–1951): an Old Bolshevik, i.e. a member of the Bolshevik Party from before 1917. Soviet ambassador to the USA from 1941 to 1943.

MIRRA LOKHVITSKAYA (1869–1905): Teffi's older sister Maria, greatly admired during her lifetime for her often boldly erotic poetry. Teffi wrote surprisingly seldom about Mirra; it is possible that she always felt in some way overshadowed by her.

ANATOLY LUNACHARSKY (1875–1933): a leading Bolshevik; after the Revolution, the first People's Commissar for Culture and Education.

MARTYN MANDELSTAM (1872–1947): a journalist; later a Soviet functionary.

DMITRY MEREZHKOVSKY (1865–1941): a Symbolist poet and novelist, married to Zinaida Gippius. He was nominated nine times for the Nobel Prize for Literature.

NIKOLAI MINSKY (1855–1937): a minor poet, close to Merezhkovsky and Gippius.

VLADIMIR NEMIROVICH-DANCHENKO (1858–1943): a theatre critic, playwright and director; co-founder, with Konstantin Stanislavsky, of the Moscow Art Theatre.

NATALYA NORDMAN-SEVEROVA (1863–1914): a writer; Ilya Repin's second wife.

JÓZEF KLEMENS PIŁSUDSKI (1867–1935): a Polish statesman, the person most responsible for the creation of the Second Republic of Poland in 1918. He was Chief of State from

1918 to 1922, and the republic's de facto leader for the rest of his life.

GEORGY PLEKHANOV (1856 –1918): a Russian revolutionary and one of the first Russian Marxists.

STANISLAV PROPPER (c.1853–1931): an Austrian immigrant, he acquired the *Stock Exchange Gazette* in 1880. After the Bolshevik Revolution, he emigrated to Germany.

ALEXEI REMIZOV (1877–1957): a Symbolist, almost surrealist, writer whose work drew on Russian folklore and old Russian literature. He emigrated to Berlin in 1921, and to Paris in 1923.

ILYA REPIN (1844–1930): probably the greatest of all Russian realist painters.

VASILY ROZANOV (1856–1919): a highly controversial writer and philosopher. His best work is deeply personal, much of it an attempt to reconcile Christian teachings with an assertion of the importance of sexuality and family life. His emphasis on the phallus has led to his being referred to as "the Rasputin of the Russian intelligentsia" (Klaus von Beyme, *Politische Theorien im Zeitalter der Ideologien*, Wiesbaden 2002, pp. 604–05). Himself a somewhat Dostoevskian figure, he married Polina Suslova, a woman twice his age who had once been Dostoevsky's mistress. In 1919 he died of starvation.

PYOTR RUMYANTSEV (1859–1929): a colleague of Lenin's in 1905, he abandoned politics two years later.

SKITALETS, "the Wanderer" (1869–1941): the son of a former serf, he was a poet and writer, and a disciple of Gorky, whom he first met in 1897.

DIOMID TOPURIDZE (1871–1942), also known by his pseudonym Karsky: a Georgian Menshevik.

VERGEZHSKY, pseudonym of Ariadna Tyrkova-Williams (1869–1962): a Russian journalist, founder member of the Constitutional Democrat (*Kadet*) party and a campaigner for women's rights.

LUDMILA VILKINA-MINSKAYA (1873–1920): a poet, Minsky's second wife.

MARKO VOVCHOK (1833–1907): pseudonym of Maria Vilinska, who wrote in both Ukrainian and Russian. Her acclaimed volume of Ukrainian folk tales was translated into Russian by Ivan Turgenev.

ANNA VYRUBOVA (1884–1964): a close friend of the Tsaritsa and an intermediary between Rasputin and the royal family. She was also a childhood friend of Prince Felix Yusupov, who played a major role in the plot to murder Rasputin.

BORIS VYSHESLAVTSEV (1877–1954): a Russian philosopher and religious thinker.

PRINCE FELIX YUSUPOV (1887–1967): married the niece of the last tsar. He was one of the three participants in the murder of Rasputin, on 30th December 1916, in the Yusupov Palace.

THE ZAITSEVS: the family of the writer Boris Zaitsev (1881–1972), who emigrated from Russia to Paris in 1922. Teffi was, for many years, close to the whole family and was particularly fond of Natasha, the young daughter who is the central character of "The White Flower". In a letter to Boris Zaitsev from around September 1925 Teffi wrote: "As for my tenderness toward you, never doubt it, because it's organic. Not only spiritual, but bodily. We are of the same tribe… Our blood, the smell of our skin, its color, our soft hair, everything is of the same sort—our own" (Edith Haber, forthcoming biography of Teffi, chapter 7). In the Russian text of "The White Flower" Teffi refers to the Zaitsevs merely by their initial: "Z".

VLADIMIR ZLOBIN (1894–1967): the Merezhkovskys' secretary and closest friend. He left Russia together with them in 1919 and he shared an apartment with them in Paris. After their deaths he took care of their archive and wrote a memoir, *Difficult Soul* (*Tyazhelaya Dusha*), about Zinaida Gippius.

Acknowledgements

I. RUSSIAN TEXTS:

"How I Live and Work" was published in the illustrated magazine *Illyustrirovannaya Rossiya* (Paris), 27th February 1926; never republished since.

"My Pseudonym" was first published in the newspaper *Vozrozhdenie* (Paris), 20th December 1931. Republished in *Moya Letopis'*.

"My First Visit to an Editorial Office" was first published in the journal *Segodnya* (Riga), 29th September 1929; included in the collection of memoirs *Moya Letopis'* (Moscow: Vagrius, 2004).

"Liza" was first published in the short story collection *Gorodok*, (Paris, 1927); reprinted in *Izbrannye proizvedeniya* (Moscow: Lakom, 1999), vol. 3.

"Love" was first published in *Illyustrirovannaya Rossiya*, 15th November 1924, then in *Gorodok*; reprinted in *Izbrannye proizvedeniya*, vol. 3.

"The Green Devil" was first published in *Segodnya* (Riga), 25th December 1925, then in *Gorodok*; reprinted in *Izbrannye proizvedeniya*, vol. 3.

"Valya" was first published in *Vozrozhdenie* (Paris), 7th January 1926, then in *Gorodok*; reprinted in *Izbrannye proizvedeniya*, vol. 3.

"Staging Posts" was first published in *Poslednie novosti* (Paris), 28th April 1940, then in *Zemnaya Raduga* (New York: Chekhov Publishing House, 1952); reprinted in *Izbrannye proizvedeniya*, vol. 3.

"The White Flower" was first published in *Zveno* (Paris), 3rd March 1924, then in *Gorodok*; reprinted in *Izbrannye proizvedeniya*, vol. 3.

"New Life": The first part, up to "And so I began waiting for Lenin", was published in the newspaper *Novoe russkoe slovo* (New York), 25th June 1950, under the title "45 Years". The entire article was later republished in *Vozrozhdenie* (Paris), January and February 1956, nos. 49 and 50. Teffi almost certainly intended this as a single article, titled *"New Life"*, though recent Russian editions, including *Moya Letopis'*, still publish it as two separate articles: "45 Years" and *"New Life"*. Reprinted in *Moya Letopis'*.

"Rasputin" was first published in *Segodnya* on 10th, 13th and 14th August 1924, then in *Vospominaniya* (Paris, 1932); reprinted in *Moya Letopis'*.

"We Are Still Living" may not have been published in Teffi's lifetime. Included in *Kontrrevolyutsionnaya bukva* (St Petersburg: Azbuka, 2006) and *Teffi v strane vospominanii* (Kiev: LP Media, 2011).

"The Gadarene Swine" was first published in *Gryadushchy Den'* (Odessa), March 1919; reprinted in *Kontrrevolyutsionnaya bukva* and *Teffi v strane vospominanii*.

"My First Tolstoy" was first published in *Poslednie novosti* (Paris), 21st November 1920.

"The Merezhkovskys" was first published in *Novoe russkoe slovo* (New York), 29 January 1950; reprinted in *Moya Letopis'*.

"Ilya Repin" was first published in *Moya Letopis'* from a manuscript in RGALI (Russian State Archive of Literature and Art).

2.

Earlier versions of these translations have been published as follows: "Rasputin" and "My First Tolstoy" in *Subtly Worded* (London: Pushkin Press, 2014); "Love" in *Russian Short Stories from Pushkin to Buida* (London: Penguin Classics, 2005).

3.

Thank you to the following, who have all either helped check the English texts or answer questions about the original:

ACKNOWLEDGEMENTS

Tamara Alexandrova, Maria Bloshteyn, Ilona Chavasse, Olive Classe, Jane Costlow, Kathryn Davies, Boris Dralyuk, Alexandra Fleming, Paul Gallagher, Anna Gunin, Anne Gutt, Edythe Haber, Nicky Harman, Rosalind Harvey, Sara Jolly, Elena Malysheva, Steve Marder, Melanie Mauthner, Olga Meerson, Melanie Moore, Alexander Nakhimovsky, Natasha Perova, Anna Pilkington, Joseph Prestwich, Donald Rayfield, Richard Shaw, Yevgeny Slivkin, Irina Steinberg, Elena Trubilova, Elena Volkova, Maria Wiltshire, Christine Worobec, and many other members of two invaluable mail groups—the Emerging Translators' Network and SEELANGS.

Notes

HOW I LIVE AND WORK

1   A common French idiom. Here, the sense is "Well, that's just too bad."

MY PSEUDONYM

1   Taffy is the name of a young British art student in *Trilby*, a novel by George du Maurier; it is also the name of a young girl in one of Rudyard Kipling's *Just So Stories*. And "Taffy was a Welshman" is the first line of a well-known English nursery rhyme. Teffi gives these two lines in English, misquoting and misspelling as here. She is, presumably, reproducing how she used to say these lines as a child. In this apparently autobiographical article Teffi is, as always, being playful. In reality, she first used the pseudonym "Teffi" as early as 1901, six years before the first performances of *The Woman Question* (Elena Trubilova, in *Na ostrove moikh vospominanii* (Tikhvin, 2016), p. 12).

2   Not all English vowel sounds have exact Russian equivalents. The standard Russian transliteration of "Taffy" is "Тэффи" (Teffi).

MY FIRST VISIT TO AN EDITORIAL OFFICE

1   It is unclear whether Teffi had one or two elder brothers. There is documentary evidence only for one elder brother, Nikolai Lokhvitsky

(1867–1933), who attended military school and by the end of the First
Word War had attained the rank of lieutenant general. Here, however,
we have an elder brother attending a lycée rather than a military school
and there are two other stories ("Love" and "The Scarecrow") in which
Nikolai is presented as the second of two brothers (Haber, chapter
1). The biographical truth is, at present, impossible to establish with
certainty. On the one hand, Teffi presents her stories simply as stories,
not as biographical memoirs; on the other hand, it is odd that she so
often mentions having two brothers.

2 Typically a peasant woman employed first as a wet-nurse to a baby
and then kept on as a household servant. Often she was more deeply
involved with a child's life than its mother.

3 The illustrated journal *Sever* (*The North*), founded in 1887.

4 Nadezhda Lokhvitskaya studied in the Liteiny Girls' School in
Mokhovaya Street, St Petersburg. The school celebrated its twentieth
jubilee in 1884. The Tsaritsa would have been Maria Fyodorovna, wife
of Alexander III.

5 Journals of the time often had a "post bag", a section where authors
of manuscripts submitted for approval were publicly offered advice
and criticism.

LIZA

1 When Teffi was a child, her family—like many upper-class Russian
families—spent each autumn and winter in St Petersburg and each
spring and summer in their country estate. In their case, this was Teffi's
mother's estate, in Volhynia, in what is now Western Ukraine—a
remote and exotic area at this time even for Russians. The children
saw little of the families of other landowners, most of whom were
Poles, and had more contact with ordinary villagers. Teffi appears to
have been the fifth child in the family and to have felt closest to Lena,
her youngest sister.

2 For Orthodox Christians, the day before Easter Sunday—the day
Christ descended into Hell—is a day of fasting and mourning. The
last service of the day, the Easter Vigil, reaches its climax at midnight,
with the celebration of Christ's resurrection.

LOVE

1   He is probably limping in imitation of Lord Byron. For more on Teffi's brother(s), see "My First Visit to an Editorial Office", note 1.

2   A *baba* is a peasant woman; neckweed is another name for hemp.

3   In her autobiographical sketch "Kishmish", Teffi explains that a *kishmish* is a kind of small raisin from the Caucasus and that she was given this nickname because, until she suddenly grew quite tall towards the age of thirteen, she was exceptionally short. Her shortness—and this nickname—greatly upset her.

4   *Martha, or Richmond Fair* (1847) by the German composer Friedrich von Flotow (1812–83).

5   The heroine of many Russian folk tales, here confused with Helen of Troy.

THE GREEN DEVIL

1   See "Love", note 3.

2   Twenty years later, in 1947, Teffi ended her article about Baba Yaga, the archetypal old witch of Russian folk tales, with an almost identical single word paragraph: "B-o-r-i-n-g" ("*Sku-u-uchno*"). She was clearly alluding to this story, which ends with the same word. As an adolescent Teffi wanted to be a Cleopatra; in 1947, in her mid-seventies, she sees herself as Baba Yaga. See Robert Chandler, *Russian Magic Tales from Pushkin to Platonov* (London: Penguin Classics 2012). In this translation we have drawn the word out, in order to lend it the appropriate emotional weight; Teffi draws the word out in her 1947 article, but not in "The Green Devil" itself.

VALYA

1   Teffi was young when she had her first child, but not as young as this implies. She married in January 1892 and, aged twenty, gave birth to her daughter Valeria in November that year. Her marriage was deeply unhappy and Teffi eventually abandoned her husband and children, returning to St Petersburg and soon beginning to earn her living as a professional writer.

2   A department store in Moscow run from 1880 to 1918 by two Scottish businessmen, on the site of what is now the Central Department Store (TsUM) on Theatre Square. "Dresden ornaments" were, for the main part, produced between 1890 and 1910. They were made from cardboard, dampened to make it flexible, and then gilded, silvered or painted.

STAGING POSTS

1   In this story Liza represents Teffi herself, while Katya is Teffi's younger sister Lena.

2   Kulich is a sort of spiced Easter bread and *paskha* is a curd cheesecake.

3   *Baba* is not only a colloquial Russian word for a woman but also a type of cake.

4   A reference to the biblical story of Nebuchadnezzar, King of Babylon: when Shadrach, Meshach and Abednego refused to worship him, he had them thrown into a fiery furnace.

5   Masha represents Teffi's elder sister Mirra Lokhvitskaya, later a well-known poet.

6   A reference to Peter's denial of Christ. During the Last Supper Jesus predicted that, before the cock crowed the following morning, Peter would deny all knowledge of him. Liza is attending the Holy Thursday service "The Twelve Gospels of the Passion of Our Lord and Saviour Jesus Christ"—a reading of twelve passages from the Gospels relating the betrayal, arrest, trial and crucifixion of Jesus. The service also includes a procession that re-enacts Christ carrying his cross to Golgotha.

7   A famous romance composed by Yelizaveta Kochubey (1821–97).

8   This last section of the story evidently takes place during the Russian Civil War. After being evacuated from Odessa in April 1919, Teffi was on board a small ship bound for Novorossiisk, the Black Sea port from which she soon afterwards set off for Constantinople. For a more extensive treatment of this episode see Teffi, *Memories*, chapters 17–23, esp. 23.

THE WHITE FLOWER

1   This story is set in the 1920s, when Teffi was living in Paris.

2   A Russian literary journal published in Paris from 1920 to 1940.

3   Soon after the October Revolution there was an official reform of the Russian alphabet, the aim being to simplify the spelling. Many émigré publications, however, continued to use the old orthography for several more decades.

4   A pacifist Christian sect, the Dukhobors rejected both the tsarist regime and the Orthodox Church. Many emigrated to Canada in the early twentieth century.

5   Here Teffi touches on controversies within Russian Orthodoxy. Earlier in the story one of the speakers casually equated Lenin with Judas. Praying for Judas is considered a sin, in part because he was a suicide, but more importantly because of his role in condemning God to death. Lenin, like Judas, may be considered a traitor, but that is not relevant to the question of whether or not one should pray for him. Most White Russians, naturally, would have found it hard to bring themselves to pray for Lenin. Natasha's desire—or rather need—to pray for him is an indication of her extraordinary open-heartedness; it may also be Teffi's delicate way of hinting to the émigré community that it is better not to identify matters of faith with matters of political ideology.

NEW LIFE

1   Russia's defeat in this war (1904–05) further undermined the authority of the already unstable regime.

2   *Volna*, first published in March 1906.

3   A play by the Austrian writer Arthur Schnitzler.

4   A radical satirical journal produced by the journalist Nikolai Shebuev in 1905–06. The back page of the first issue carried a photograph of the Tsar's "October Manifesto" with a bloody handprint across it and the caption "Major General Trepov had a hand in this document". Trepov had played an important role in the suppression of the many strikes and rebellions that swept Russia in 1905. Only five issues of the journal were printed. Shebuev was arrested and sentenced to a year's imprisonment.

5   *Wheatfield* (*Niva*) was an illustrated weekly journal. It presented a wide selection of good quality literature to a broad readership.

6 The word "bison" (*zubr*) came to be used to refer to reactionary members of the Duma (the Russian parliament) drawn from the landowning classes. The nickname hints at an analogy between the official protection afforded such figures and the conservation of "endangered species" close to extinction. (With thanks to Boris Dralyuk for help with this note.

7 Konstantin Platonov, son of Senator S.F. Platonov.

8 The Russian Social Democratic Party was a revolutionary socialist party formed in 1898. In 1903 it split into two factions: the Bolsheviks (led by Lenin) and the Mensheviks.

9 "One Step Forward, Two Steps Back (The Crisis in our Party)", was published in Geneva in 1904.

10 After a period of internal exile in Russia, Lenin had left for Geneva in 1900. At the time Switzerland was something of a hotbed of radicalism—a number of Russian revolutionaries studied at the universities of Geneva and Zurich.

11 *Stock Exchange Gazette* (*Birzhevye vedemosti*) was a liberal St Petersburg paper to which Teffi was a regular contributor. In 1917 it was closed by the Bolsheviks.

12 This plan by the mayor of St Petersburg, P. Lelyanov, to fill in the Catherine Canal (Yekaterinsky Canal, now the Griboyedov Canal) was never put into effect.

13 In his introduction to Marx's *The Class Struggle in France* (1895), Engels describes barricade battles and armed insurrections as "obsolete" and all too likely to end in failure.

14 *New Life* (*Novaya Zhizn'*), the first legal Bolshevik newspaper, was published in St Petersburg from 27th October until 3rd December 1905.

15 The tsarist security service, the Okhrana, made extensive use of secret agents, both to gather information and to subvert revolutionary groups from within.

16 A Russian Orthodox workers' organization. In January 1905 a peaceful workers' demonstration led by Father Gapon ended with the Imperial Guard firing on demonstrators, killing about 200 people and wounding about 800. The day went down in history as "Bloody Sunday".

17 *Life Questions* (*Voprosy Zhizni*) a literary and philosophical journal.

18 Linyov worked on *Stock Exchange Gazette* between 1893 and 1896; this episode thus appears to have taken place before Teffi's involvement with *New Life*. Gorky, however, only moved to St Petersburg in 1899. Teffi's account may be inaccurate.

19 To start a newspaper, one required official permission from the Ministry of the Interior.

20 Clearly Minsky's poem had some success. There is at least one account of an educated person being convinced that it was Minsky, rather than Marx, who first came up with the phrase "Workers of the World Unite" (Korney Chukovsky, diary entry for 13th September 1927, in *Dnevnik 1901–1929* by Korney Chukovsky (Moscow: Sovremenny pisatel, 1997), pp. 413–4).

21 The title of the original is "Plehve and his Chaff" (*"Pleve i ego pleveli"*). Viacheslav von Plehve (1846–1904), Russian Minister of the Interior, was assassinated in 1904 in St Petersburg by a terrorist bomb.

22 As Governor of St Petersburg, Trepov played an important part in suppressing the 1905 Revolution. See *"New Life"*, note 4.

23 A strike by railway workers, one of the many rebellions and strikes that swept the country in 1905.

24 An anonymous popular song from the time of the French revolution, a rallying cry for revolutionaries.

25 Any activities considered subversive, including publishing inflammatory political material, could lead to a spell of internal exile. Those found guilty of serious crimes were sent to Siberia; being sent to a provincial town like Oryol was a lesser punishment.

26 Misquoted from a poem by Nikolai Nekrasov, "The Forgotten Village" (1864). This describes peasants waiting in vain for the master to come and sort out their problems.

27 Sonia Marmeladova: the young heroine of *Crime and Punishment*, who sacrifices her honour by becoming a prostitute to save her family. Sonia's appearance in the novel is described as follows: "... strange was her sudden appearance in this room, amidst the beggary, rags, death and despair. She too wore rags; her get-up was cheap, but it came with all the adornments of the street, as the rules and etiquette of that special world demanded, with its shamingly flagrant purpose. [...] She'd quite forgotten about her fourth-hand, colourful silk dress, utterly out of place here with its ridiculously long train, and about her enormous

crinoline obstructing the doorway, and her bright shoes and her parasol, which she'd taken with her even though it was night, and the ridiculous round straw hat with a feather the colour of fire." (Dostoevsky, *Crime and Punishment*, tr. Oliver Ready (London: Penguin Classics, 2014).) Teffi's implication is that the girl with Gusev is also a prostitute.

28 A reference to a pamphlet by Lenin. See *"New Life"*, note 9.

29 An ultra-nationalist Russian movement that supported the tsarist principles of Orthodoxy, Autocracy and nationality and was fiercely hostile to both revolutionaries and Jews. Its members were drawn from a variety of social classes.

30 "The Union of the Russian People", one of the Black Hundred groups, met regularly at the Tver café in St Petersburg, offering free tea and food to unemployed workers.

31 The term "pogrom" was most often used of mass acts of violence against Jews. Jews and revolutionaries, however, were often conflated, especially in the minds of the Black Hundreds and other extreme nationalists.

32 The article in question, "The Dying Autocracy and the New Organs of Party Rule", was published in November 1905. Minsky was arrested and released on bail.

33 Russian external passports of this period included several pages intended for foreign border guards. Written in French, German and English, these stated the traveller's name and social class. (With thanks to Yevgeny Slivkin.)

34 In 1917, after the February Revolution and the abdication of the Tsar, the Provisional Government continued the war against Germany. Wanting to destabilize the Russian war effort, the German government provided Lenin with a sealed railway carriage and a large sum of money, enabling him to make his way from neutral Switzerland, across Germany, and into Russia. The Bolsheviks were, at the time, the only Russian political party unambiguously committed to making peace with Germany.

RASPUTIN

1 "Madame V——" probably refers to Anna Vyrubova (see *List of Historical Figures*). Elsewhere in this memoir Teffi refers to her by name, but this may well be a minor inconsistency on her part.

2 Grigory (or Grisha) Rasputin is often referred to as a monk, but he never took holy orders and had no official connection to the Orthodox Church. Here Teffi uses the vaguer term "elder". Rasputin was also rumoured to have belonged to an extreme sect known as the Khlysts, but this has never been proven. There is no doubt, however, that he lived the life of a religious "wanderer" for several years and was widely believed to be endowed with healing powers.

3 Often the subject of lurid speculation, the Khlysts observed ascetic practices and ecstatic rituals as a way of attaining grace.

4 A town fifteen miles from the centre of St Petersburg, the location of the Russian royal family's summer palace.

5 After its acquisition by Alexey Suvorin in 1876, *New Times* (*Novoye Vremya*) became one of the most successful papers in Russia. Though reactionary and anti-Semitic, it published some of Russia's most important writers, including Anton Chekhov.

6 The Orthodox term for the women who, early in the morning of the third day, came to Christ's tomb and found it empty.

7 Alexey Filippov was a banker and the publisher of writings by Rasputin. Ivan Manasevich-Manuilov was a police agent. According to Edward Radzinsky, Manasevich-Manuilov had "suggested that Filippov organize a literary soirée, and he himself had told Tsarskoye Selo about the soirée, attributing the initiative to Filippov. And he had passed on to the security branch [...] the list of literary invitees. All the people on it were well-known 'leftist writers'. Which was why there had been a call from Tsarskoye Selo interrupting the meeting" (*Rasputin: The Last Word* (London: Phoenix, 2000), p. 403). Manasevich-Manuilov had evidently wanted to compromise Filippov both in the eyes of the authorities and in the eyes of Rasputin himself. In the original, Teffi refers to Filippov and Manasevich-Manuilov only by their initial letters.

WE ARE STILL LIVING

1 A *tulup* is a large sheepskin coat, usually worn by men. A *zipun* is a coat that flares from the waist, often seen as typically Cossack.

2 Shortly before the October Revolution the Bolsheviks made the Smolny, previously a government building, into their administrative headquarters.

3 Kangaroo was one of the furs used in military uniforms in Russia, together with squirrel and sheepskin. Ordinary soldiers usually had sheepskin collars.

4 A phrase used by Lenin to refer to the distribution of capital.

5 A term used in Marxist theory to describe the abandonment, as capitalism developed, of the collective solidarity characteristic of feudalism.

6 See *"New Life"*, note 31. Though most often used of right-wing violence against Jews, this term was also used of murderous rampages by revolutionary crowds.

7 Patriarch Nikon, the head of the Russian Orthodox Church, pronounced an anathema on the Bolsheviks in January 1918.

8 Bread rationing was introduced by the Provisional Government in March 1917, and bread continued to be rationed—as well as being adulterated with other substances—under "War Communism" (1918–21). In *The Black Notebooks* (her diary of the post-revolutionary period), Zinaida Gippius writes that "the ration of bread 'with straw' is ⅛ of a pound", i.e. a little under two ounces per person (entry for February 1918).

THE GADARENE SWINE

1 See *"New Life"*, note 29.

2 An allusion to Genesis vii, where God tells Noah, "Of every clean beast thou shalt take to thee by sevens, the male and the female: and of beasts that are not clean by two, the male and the female." In the biblical story, the beasts do *not* devour one another.

THE MEREZHKOVSKYS

1 A reference to Bely's "Memories of Blok", published in Berlin in 1922–23. Merezhkovsky's habit of wearing carpet slippers with pompoms is mentioned by several other memoirists.

2 From Nikolai Gogol's story "Viy".

3 In June 1940, as the German army advanced on Paris, around three quarters of the city's population fled in panic. Many of the Russian émigrés went to Biarritz, though this too was soon under German occupation.

4 Merezhkovsky turned seventy-five on 14th August 1940. Zlobin writes in *Difficult Soul* that, to help them financially, their friends organized a birthday celebration which turned a profit of 7,000 francs.

5 Sobakyevich, an unscrupulous serf owner in Gogol's *Dead Souls*, who, despite his name (*sobaka* is the Russian for "dog"), resembles a bear.

6 *Witch*, a collection of stories with themes drawn from folklore and the supernatural, was published in 1936.

7 From Gogol's "A Theatrical Journey" ("*Teatralny razezd*"), written in response to critics of his play *The Government Inspector*.

8 Teffi is referring to Merezhkovsky's early poem "Sakya Muni" (1885), in which a poor thief berates the Buddha for preventing him from stealing one of the Buddha's gems: the Buddha is immortal and has no need of gems—so why should he deny a mortal thief a way to earn his crust of bread?

9 Throughout his émigré years Merezhkovsky had been hoping to find a strong ruler who could save Europe from Bolshevism. At one time he had placed his hopes in Mussolini, who had sponsored his book about Dante (1939). Merezhkovsky met Mussolini several times. In one of his letters to him he wrote, "The best, the truest and the liveliest document on Dante is—your personality. [...] Visualize Mussolini in contemplation, and it's Dante. Imagine Dante in action, and it's Mussolini" (Vadim Polonsky, "Merezhkovsky, Dmitry Sergeyevich", www.krugosvet.ru; retrieved 2nd February 2010).

ILYA REPIN

1 In 1910 this publishing house (Shipovnik) had published Teffi's first two books—a collection of poems and a collection of stories.

2 First published in December 1915—a story about an exceptionally fatuous man whose repeated expressions of wonder at life's everyday miracles bore and exasperate not only his wife but also his small children.

3 All four artists emigrated after the Revolution. Teffi's *Memories* includes a brief mention of Schleifer and longer mentions of Yakovlev. The whereabouts of these portraits are unknown; probably they have not survived.

4   Teffi seems unaware of any distinction between vegetarianism and veganism—a distinction perhaps seldom made at this time.

5   Teffi also tells this story in chapter 2 of *Memories*; some details differ.

6   Then one of the north-western provinces of the Russian empire, now a part of Lithuania—Kovno in Russian, Kaunas in Lithuanian.

7   In 1951 Teffi sent the manuscript of *My Chronicle*, her collection of short memoirs about writers and other important figures she had known, to the Chekhov Publishing House in New York. The book was not published and the manuscript she sent is now lost. It is, however, possible to establish the titles of many of the articles included—many of them already published in journals. The last paragraph of this memoir of Repin suggests that this piece was intended as a conclusion to the book as a whole.

Pushkin Press

Pushkin Press was founded in 1997, and publishes novels, essays, memoirs, children's books—everything from timeless classics to the urgent and contemporary.

Our books represent exciting, high-quality writing from around the world: we publish some of the twentieth century's most widely acclaimed, brilliant authors such as Stefan Zweig, Marcel Aymé, Antal Szerb, Gaito Gazdanov and Yasushi Inoue, as well as compelling and award-winning contemporary writers, including Andrés Neuman, Edith Pearlman, Erwin Mortier and Ayelet Gundar-Goshen.

Pushkin Press publishes the world's best stories, to be read and read again. Here are just some of the titles from our long and varied list. For more amazing stories, visit www.pushkinpress.com.

THE SPECTRE OF ALEXANDER WOLF

GAITO GAZDANOV

'A mesmerising work of literature' Antony Beevor

BINOCULAR VISION

EDITH PEARLMAN

'A genius of the short story' Mark Lawson, *Guardian*

IN THE BEGINNING WAS THE SEA

TOMÁS GONZÁLEZ

'Smoothly intriguing narrative, with its touches of sinister, Patricia Highsmith-like menace' *Irish Times*

BEWARE OF PITY

STEFAN ZWEIG

'Zweig's fictional masterpiece' *Guardian*

TRAVELLER OF THE CENTURY

ANDRÉS NEUMAN

'A beautiful, accomplished novel: as ambitious as it is generous, as moving as it is smart' Juan Gabriel Vásquez, *Guardian*

THE WORLD OF YESTERDAY

STEFAN ZWEIG

'*The World of Yesterday* is one of the greatest memoirs of the twentieth century, as perfect in its evocation of the world Zweig loved, as it is in its portrayal of how that world was destroyed' David Hare

WAKE UP, SIR!

JONATHAN AMES

'The novel is extremely funny but it is also sad and poignant, and almost incredibly clever' *Guardian*

BONITA AVENUE

PETER BUWALDA

'One wild ride: a swirling helix of a family saga… a new writer as toe-curling as early Roth, as roomy as Franzen and as caustic as Houellebecq' *Sunday Telegraph*

JOURNEY BY MOONLIGHT

ANTAL SZERB

'Just divine… makes you imagine the author has had private access to your own soul' Nicholas Lezard, *Guardian*

ONE NIGHT, MARKOVITCH

AYELET GUNDAR-GOSHEN

'Wry, ironically tinged and poignant… this is a fable for the twenty-first century' *Sunday Telegraph*

KARATE CHOP & MINNA NEEDS REHEARSAL SPACE

DORTHE NORS

'Unique in form and effect… Nors has found a novel way of getting into the human heart' *Guardian*

RED LOVE: THE STORY OF AN EAST GERMAN FAMILY

MAXIM LEO

'Beautiful and supremely touching… an unbearably poignant description of a world that no longer exists' *Sunday Telegraph*

BY BLOOD

ELLEN ULLMAN

'Delicious and intriguing' *Daily Telegraph*

THE LAST DAYS

LAURENT SEKSIK

'Mesmerising… Seksik's portrait of Zweig's final months
is dignified and tender' *Financial Times*

TALKING TO OURSELVES

ANDRÉS NEUMAN

'This is writing of a quality rarely encountered… when you read Neuman's
beautiful novel, you realise a very high bar has been set' *Guardian*

JOURNEY INTO THE PAST

STEFAN ZWEIG

'Lucid, tender, powerful and compelling' *Independent*

FROM THE FATHERLAND, WITH LOVE

RYU MURAKAMI

'If Haruki is The Beatles of Japanese literature,
Ryu is its Rolling Stones' David Pilling

THE BREAK

PIETRO GROSSI

'Small and perfectly formed… reaching its end leaves the
reader desirous to start all over again' *Independent*

COIN LOCKER BABIES

RYU MURAKAMI

'A fascinating peek into the weirdness of contemporary Japan' Oliver Stone

CLOSE TO THE MACHINE

ELLEN ULLMAN

'Astonishing… impossible to put down' *San Francisco Chronicle*

MARCEL

ERWIN MORTIER

'Aspiring novelists will be hard pressed to achieve this quality' *Time Out*